PRAISE FOR *THE LEGAL RISK MANAGEMENT HANDBOOK*

'A must-read for in-house lawyers and new general counsels. I particularly like the simple and practical guides to implement what are quite advanced legal risk management techniques.'
Simon Nasta, General Counsel, FBN Bank (UK)

'Easy to read and dares to delve not just into the practical application of the law but the world of ethics and conduct and the role of lawyers to manage such. A valuable addition to the literature on legal risk.'
Richard Moorhead, Professor of Law and Professional Ethics, Chair of Law and Professional Ethics, UCL

'Legal risk acts as a brake on the competitiveness of the US and other established markets. US businesses across all sectors must seek to understand the way they interact with law and regulation, and so stay on top of the legal risks they face. Whalley and Guzelian have provided a masterful guide for achieving these goals.'
William H Byrnes, Associate Dean, Texas A&M University School of Law; Leader of National Underwriter's Financial Advisory Publications

'Legal risk management needs to become fully integrated with the practice of law. With this book, Matthew Whalley and Chris Guzelian enable in-house lawyers to get to grips with one of the least understood areas of legal practice. A must-read for General Counsel who want to articulate the value their team delivers, for Chief Compliance Officers who want to work more effectively with legal colleagues to deliver effective regulatory compliance programmes, and for any legal practitioner who operates within or delivers services to a risk-managed environment.'
Neil Braakenburg, EMEA Head of Compliance, AIG Europe (and former UK Head of Legal, AIG Europe)

'*The Legal Risk Management Handbook* contains a wealth of information useful for any company involved in international business to consider when managing legal risk. What sets this book apart is that it translates complex legal principles into practical operating tools that business managers and the lawyers who work with them can use on a day-to-day basis. An indispensable compendium for the legal and compliance team, the executive suite and the boardroom who must work hard to ensure that legal risk management is at the top of the agenda in every organization.'
Professor Stuart Weinstein, Faculty of Business and Law, Coventry University, and Consulting Editor, *Legal Risk Management, Governance and Compliance: A guide to best practice from leading experts* (Globe Law and Business, 2013) and *Legal Risk Management, Governance and Compliance: Interdisciplinary case studies from leading experts* (Globe Law and Business, 2016)

'This book challenges all organizations to review legal risk management strategy and provides practical suggestions on how to flex their approach to enhance legislative and regulatory compliance. All those in leadership or front line advisory roles will relate to the issues raised and can benefit from the proposed solutions to manage their forward exposures to legal loss.'
Matthew Kellett, EY UK Law Leader, FSO

'Legal risk management is often still seen as a niche discipline, but I believe it has great potential once it is adopted more broadly. One of the problems is that many practitioners do not even know what this nascent discipline entails and what they should learn to start practising it. This book is a very good starting point because it offers useful practical guidelines and illustrating cases. Thanks to their professional experiences with practising legal risk management, the authors are uniquely qualified for offering such guidance.'
Professor Tobias Mahler, Norwegian Research Center for Computers and Law, Faculty of Law, University of Oslo

'In-house legal teams are facing major challenges. We need more books like this.'
Ashley Gordon, Head of Legal, EMEA

The Legal Risk Management Handbook

An international guide to protect your business from legal loss

Matthew Whalley
Chris Guzelian

KoganPage

First published in Great Britain and the United States in 2017 by Kogan Page Limited

2nd Floor, 45 Gee Street
London EC1V 3RS
United Kingdom
www.koganpage.com

c/o Martin P Hill Consulting
122 W 27th St, 10th Floor
New York NY 10001
USA

4737/23 Ansari Road
Daryaganj
New Delhi 110002
India

ISBN 978 0 7494 7797 4
E-ISBN 978 0 7494 7798 1

British Library Cataloguing-in-Publication Data

A CIP record for this book is available from the British Library.

Library of Congress Cataloging-in-Publication Data

Names: Whalley, Matthew, author. | Guzelian, Chris, author.
Title: The legal risk management handbook : an international guide to protect your business from legal loss / Matthew Whalley, Chris Guzelian.
Description: London ; New York : Kogan Page Limited, 2016. | Includes bibliographical references and index.
Identifiers: LCCN 2016040487 (print) | LCCN 2016040676 (ebook) | ISBN 9780749477974 (alk. paper) | ISBN 9780749477981 (ebook)
Subjects: LCSH: International business enterprises–Law and legislation. | Corporate governance–Law and legislation. | Risk management–Law and legislation.
Classification: LCC K1322 .W43 2016 (print) | LCC K1322 (ebook) | DDC 340.068/1–dc23
LC record available at https://lccn.loc.gov/2016040487

Typeset by Graphicraft Limited, Hong Kong
Print production managed by Jellyfish
Printed and bound by CPI Group (UK) Ltd, Croydon, CR0 4YY

The Legal Risk Management Handbook

An international guide to protect your business from legal loss

Matthew Whalley
Chris Guzelian

KoganPage

Publisher's note

Every possible effort has been made to ensure that the information contained in this book is accurate at the time of going to press, and the publisher and authors cannot accept responsibility for any errors or omissions, however caused. No responsibility for loss or damage occasioned to any person acting, or refraining from action, as a result of the material in this publication can be accepted by the editor, the publisher or any of the authors.

First published in Great Britain and the United States in 2017 by Kogan Page Limited

2nd Floor, 45 Gee Street
London EC1V 3RS
United Kingdom
www.koganpage.com

c/o Martin P Hill Consulting
122 W 27th St, 10th Floor
New York NY 10001
USA

4737/23 Ansari Road
Daryaganj
New Delhi 110002
India

ISBN 978 0 7494 7797 4
E-ISBN 978 0 7494 7798 1

British Library Cataloguing-in-Publication Data

A CIP record for this book is available from the British Library.

Library of Congress Cataloging-in-Publication Data

Names: Whalley, Matthew, author. | Guzelian, Chris, author.
Title: The legal risk management handbook : an international guide to protect your business from legal loss / Matthew Whalley, Chris Guzelian.
Description: London ; New York : Kogan Page Limited, 2016. | Includes bibliographical references and index.
Identifiers: LCCN 2016040487 (print) | LCCN 2016040676 (ebook) | ISBN 9780749477974 (alk. paper) | ISBN 9780749477981 (ebook)
Subjects: LCSH: International business enterprises–Law and legislation. | Corporate governance–Law and legislation. | Risk management–Law and legislation.
Classification: LCC K1322 .W43 2016 (print) | LCC K1322 (ebook) | DDC 340.068/1–dc23
LC record available at https://lccn.loc.gov/2016040487

Typeset by Graphicraft Limited, Hong Kong
Print production managed by Jellyfish
Printed and bound by CPI Group (UK) Ltd, Croydon, CR0 4YY

CONTENTS

ABOUT THE CONTRIBUTORS

We couldn't have written this book without the generosity and insights of our contributors and interviewees. We want you to know whose thoughts and words we have combined with our own when we wrote each chapter. We owe particular thanks to those people who sat down to write several thousand words on our behalf: Deven Desai (Chapter 8), Georgi Dimitrov (Chapter 7), Martin Loenstrup (Chapter 6), Parminder Nahl (Chapter 2), Michael Redman (Chapter 7), Nick Rowles-Davies (Chapter 7), Mel Schwarz (Chapter 4), Magnus Steen (Chapter 6) and Ben Terner (Chapter 6).

Insights have also been derived via interview and conversation from: Mark Beer OBE (Chapter 7), Laurent Calvet (Chapter 3) Graeme Copnell (Chapters 2 and 5), Joe Grundfest (Chapters 2, 4 and 5), Tessa Hastie (Chapter 2), Richard Moorhead (Chapter 5), Oliver Rule (Chapter 7) and Philip Wood QC (Chapters 2, 4 and 5). We would also like to thank Tobias Mahler (Associate Professor of Law, University of Oslo), Richard Moorhead (Professor of Law, UCL), Dr Graeme Copnell (Senior Lecturer, UEL), Oliver Rule, Neil Braakenburg and Vas Hanumadass for their insightful and challenging review of our early drafts, and of course our team at Kogan Page: Jenny, Anna, Amy, David *et al.*

Deven Desai, Associate Professor (Georgia Institute of Technology)
Deven is an Associate Professor of Law and Ethics at the Georgia Institute of Technology, Scheller College of Business. Prior to joining Scheller, Deven was an Associate Professor of Law. He was also the first, and to date only Academic Research Counsel at Google, Inc., and a Visiting Fellow at Princeton University's Center for Information Technology Policy. Deven's scholarship examines how business interests, new technology and economic theories shape intellectual property and privacy law and where those arguments explain

productivity or where they fail to capture society's interest in the free flow of information and development.

Georgi Dimitrov, Managing Partner (Georgi Dimitrov Attorneys)
Georgi is a Managing Partner of Georgi Dimitrov Attorneys, established in 1997. In addition to his legal work, Georgi is a legal publisher of some of the most important laws with commentaries and a creative director of the Legal Risk Conference held in Skopje and Belgrade. Georgi's contribution to the quantitative analysis of dispute success is far more advanced than that outlined in this book.

Martin Loenstrup, Senior Legal Counsel (Mærsk Oil and Gas A/S)
Martin founded the Danish Contract Management Association (DCMA) in 2006. He has worked with legal, contract management and risk management for the last 10 years, most recently within the Maersk Group. He has worked with operational contract lifecycle management in different companies and industries, and has helped to transform legal departments, implement governance models and policies, and design contract management processes and tools to improve the contract process and optimize the financial performance of procurement and the supply chain.

Parminder Nahl, Company Secretary/Senior Legal Counsel (FBN Bank (UK) Limited)
Parminder worked in private practice at a magic circle law firm in London for a number of years, specializing in leveraged finance and restructurings. He now works in-house at an established African financial institution where he is responsible for legal and corporate governance matters. Parminder studied at Corpus Christi College, University of Oxford and has written a number of articles on legal developments and trends.

Michael Redman, Director and co-head, global corporate intelligence, asset tracing and enforcement business (Burford Capital)
Mike began his career in the Lloyd's of London insurance market and later worked in West Africa in the diamond industry. He has worked in the investigations sector for well over a decade and has held senior

positions in both Moscow and London at leading global commercial intelligence companies. Mike advises clients how to get their money back in high-value disputes in the natural resources, financial services and pharmaceuticals sectors.

Nick Rowles-Davies, Managing Director (Burford Capital)
Nick literally wrote the book on litigation funding: he is the author of *Third Party Litigation Funding*, the seminal work published by Oxford University Press in 2014. A pioneer in the development of the litigation funding industry in the UK and the common law world, he has led its transformation into a broad-based corporate finance offering, and has been responsible for the largest and most innovative transactions in the field, including a $45 million portfolio financing deal for a FTSE 20 company.

Mel Schwarz, Adjunct Professor (Thomas Jefferson School of Law)
Mel was a litigation associate and partner at Dechert LLP, an international law firm, for 27 years. He also served as Special Counsel for Civil Enforcement in the Antitrust Division of the US Department of Justice, where he was lead trial counsel in the case brought against Visa and MasterCard for violations of the Sherman Act and against Lockheed Martin and Northrop Grumman to enjoin their proposed merger. He was a senior in-house lawyer at Marsh & McLennan Companies, a Fortune 500 public company, and General Counsel of Guy Carpenter, a worldwide reinsurance brokerage subsidiary.

Magnus Steen, founder of Contract Business Intelligence Nordics AB
Magnus is former deputy General Counsel of Sony Ericsson. He has helped transform legal departments in leading Scandinavian companies, and advised several global companies on how to initiate cross-discipline contract management programmes. He is also part of a contract management research programme at the University of Gothenburg.

PREFACE

This book is about the legal risks that businesses need to manage. Operating within the letter and spirit of the law is a fundamental requirement for your business, but the bigger you are, the more complex this becomes. As you employ more people, conduct business in (and with) more countries, design and sell a greater range of products, to new sets of customers, you add to the chances that someone, somewhere, will do something that will break the law. The principles and practices explained in this book will help you to identify where that is most likely to happen, and put in place necessary changes to your policies, practices and procedures to minimize the chances of being on the wrong side of a legal dispute or regulatory investigation.

We write this book with the practitioner in mind, and include as many practical insights and examples of how to apply effective legal risk management as we can. Even at the most senior levels of management, you need to understand how your strategies are implemented in practice and be able to monitor their effect on corporate culture and working practices. You don't need to be a lawyer to read this book. It is not a legal textbook, descends only occasionally and where absolutely necessary into legal theory, and when we do so we do it with the non-lawyer in mind. Our strength is in the design and implementation of practical, pragmatic legal risk management solutions and it is our insight in that area that we prioritize in this book. Between us, we have 28 years' experience working in the legal sector. We have worked in legal operations, founded one of the first legal risk practices, taught the law, practised as a bankruptcy lawyer and state's attorney, worked in military intelligence, built contract robots, implemented global legal knowledge management and technology systems and accumulated a varied range of experience that qualifies us to write at least some of this book. We live in San Diego and London and have worked in UK City law firms, American Bar Association accredited law schools, global banks and leading global professional services firms.

Legal risk covers such a wide range of legal disciplines – we will define them at a high level in Chapter 1 as legislation/regulation, non-contractual obligations (duty of care/civil duty), contracts, dispute management and intellectual property (non-contractual rights) – that it would be impossible for us to write this book without guidance and contribution from other experts. We've carried out detailed interviews and received written contributions from people with brains far bigger than ours, so before you begin to read this book in earnest, we urge you to read through the 'About the Contributors' section and see whose thoughts you are reading (along with our own) in each chapter.

About this book

You will read eight chapters, which we've structured in two parts. Chapters 1–3 are management level: they outline the business case for legal risk (including what it actually is), what 'top-down' (or 'big picture') legal risk management looks like, and how to implement an effective 'bottom-up' legal risk management framework:

1 The business case for legal risk, the cost of legal risk, how to articulate legal risk to your business, and how to create a robust definition of legal risk.

2 Big picture legal risk management: corporate governance, and how to influence working practices in your organization; board-level legal risk management, the evolving role of the company secretary, and what good policy looks like.

3 Evidence you're in control: how to identify, quantify and report legal risk. How to use our five-step legal risk framework to evidence that you are in control of legal risk.

Chapters 4–8 are an in-depth review of the key issues within each of our five top-level legal risk categories:

4 Legislative/regulatory risk management: horizon scanning, legislative risk assessment, and legal/regulatory compliance; detail on

the different roles of legal and compliance and how to structure them to manage legal risk.

5 Non-contractual obligations risks: ethical interpretation of action, and the risk of failure in your duty of care; a framework to predict where regulator opinion is moving, and stay ahead of regulatory enforcement activity.
6 Contract risk management: strategic contract lifecycle management, and how to measure the key risks in your contracts; the role of contracts in your organization and how to maximize their value.
7 Dispute risk management: top tips on dispute strategies, assessment tools for likelihood of success, and discussion of options for dispute funding and recovery.
8 Non-contractual rights risk: the effects of digitization, disruption and disintermediation on different industries, and how new approaches to Intellectual Property (IP) management is putting IP at the centre of your customer strategy.

In these chapters you will read where particular risks originate, how they can bubble up to the surface, and practical steps you can take to mitigate the chances of that happening in your business. We've tried to make this book sector-agnostic, and as you will read in the war stories (or scare stories!) legal risk results in huge losses for businesses across a wide range of sectors.

The nature of the legal risks in the financial services sector, the frequency with which they are reported, and our own experience working within that sector, mean that you will find we often lean towards examples from it. Having said that, where we cover ethics and policy we use the health sector as a source of material and examples of what has worked and what hasn't. Our contributors for the chapter on contractual risk (Chapter 6) have particular experience in manufacturing, oil and gas, technology and e-business – so maybe we're not quite as biased as we think! With that thought, we hope sincerely that you will enjoy reading this handbook and, above all, that you will find one or two nuggets of gold to help you protect your own business from legal loss.

Note: All references in the text to $ refer to US dollars.

For Helen, Eva and Sylvie,
for their patience,
and Henno,
for the original thought.
Matthew Whalley

For all who toil to keep others safe.
Chris Guzelian

PART ONE
A general guide to legal risk management and reporting

The business case for legal risk 01

How to articulate legal risk to your business

Legal risk is the risk of financial or reputational loss that can result from lack of awareness or misunderstanding of, ambiguity in, or reckless indifference to, the way law and regulation apply to your business, its relationships, processes, products and services.

Introduction

Legal risk is ill-defined and poorly understood in business. Surveys carried out by international law firm Berwin Leighton Paisner in 2013 and global professional services firm Ernst & Young in 2016 provide evidence of a striking lack of confidence in understanding legal risk; and a similar lack of confidence in businesses' ability to prevent legal loss. There are many ways in which legal risk can result in legal loss, and legal losses often materialize through litigation costs and regulatory fines. Using this measure the cost of legal losses can be estimated at over $100 billion per year in just the financial services sector. Outside of financial services, businesses in the United Kingdom, United States, Brazil, Germany, Switzerland and Australia – and in energy and manufacturing, banking and insurance – have suffered billion dollar losses as a result of legal risk. In many cases the reputational damage has dwarfed the direct financial losses. Because the cost of getting legal risk wrong is so high, we believe there is a clear need for businesses across all sectors to improve their understanding, and invest in programmes to identify and manage legal risk proactively before losses are incurred.

The secret to managing legal risk proactively – and protecting your business from legal loss – is to understand where legal risk comes from. So although this book, and this chapter in particular, contains many examples and stories of how legal risk can lead to unwanted headlines and huge financial losses, at its heart we set out a system to identify, quantify and mitigate the root cause of these losses. Our system is founded on a simple definition of legal risk (above) that we will explain in full towards the end of the chapter. Our definition provides a clear scope to legal risk management in your business and grounds legal risk management in operational practice. We focus on operational practice deliberately. Although the law itself can change, and later in this book you will read how regulatory attitudes have moved ahead of common business practice in some sectors, your exposure to legal risk results from the way your business interacts with law and regulation in its current and future state.

In this chapter you will read about the cost of getting legal risk wrong. More important, you will learn the five key ways in which your business practices interact with the law, and read 18 descriptive examples that will enable you to pinpoint legal risk in your business and so take the first steps to mitigate its impact.

> Legal risk definitions are central to proactive legal risk management. They set the boundaries for your discussions with the business.

How legal risk results in financial and reputational loss

Petrobras, Volkswagen and the financial services sector

The financial cost of legal risk is indisputable. In the banking sector, legal losses cost 10 of the world's largest banks $40 billion per year over the last five years (CCP Research Foundation, 2016). As an example of why those fines were imposed, in 2014 the cumulative fines for banks involved in fixing Libor rates added up to more than $3 billion. Libor is the overnight rate used to set inter-bank lending rates in the financial markets. When traders take advantageous positions through advance knowledge of what the rate will be, it is potentially a criminal offence and for the companies involved a clear failing in their duty of care to the market. Regulators in the United Kingdom and United States imposed eye-watering fines on the banks involved in fixing the rate, and the cost of the investigations, lost revenue and legal defence added up to many more billions.

However, it isn't just financial costs that you need to worry about. The reputational damage caused by Libor and other conduct-related scandals in the wake of the financial crisis has contributed to a shift in public perception of the banks and a much tougher regulatory regime. All banks have suffered and are being required to change the way they operate, invest heavily in new structures, and be transparent about the benefit they deliver to their customers/clients. The total cost to the sector of these changes could easily add up to trillions of dollars.

Outside of the banking sector, individual losses resulting from reckless indifference to law and regulation (a core element of legal risk) can be even more eye-watering. You will read more in the next section about how Petrobras lost 62 per cent of its market value in the wake of its corruption scandal, and how the cost to Volkswagen of its 'cheat device' was reported in 2015 at around $5 billion. These two companies are also clear examples of how legal risks can damage your brand and the long-term health of your business. They also provide data that help you quantify the reputational impact of legal risk on a business, a sector or a nation.

The impact of legal risk on Petrobras and brand Brazil

Petrobras (Petroleo Brasileiro SA) is the huge state-controlled Brazilian energy company at the heart of probably Brazil's biggest corruption scandal. In March 2014 former Petrobras director Paulo Roberto Costa was arrested in connection with an investigation into alleged corruption charges. Despite vocal support for Petrobras from the Brazilian president, Dilma Roussef, in September that year Costa named government officials as being involved in the corruption. In 2015, as more details emerged, Petrobras continued to generate international headlines: prosecutors alleged that executives colluded to inflate the price of contracts, giving pay-offs to lawmakers and other officials to fund political campaigns. The immediate effect on the value of the company was significant, with a drop in market value of 62 per cent. The company replaced its executive team and created a new position of chief governance, risk and compliance officer to replace its previous chief international officer. Estimates at the time, based on a calculation of projects that were overstated, valued the cost to Petrobras of the corruption at $2 billion.

Many cases for anti-competitive behaviour are yet to be taken into account in those figures, but even so the numbers pale in comparison to the negative effect on the national brand of Brazil. Petrobras' individual contribution to direct loss of Brazilian GDP has been calculated as $27.1 billion (or 1 per cent of total GDP) (*International Finance Magazine*, 2015). This is one of a number of corruption scandals that contributed to a 17 per cent drop ($230 billion) in the Brazilian nation's brand value in 2015. This is despite the fact that Brazil hosted/was preparing to host two of the most brand-enhancing world events – the 2014 World Cup and 2016 Olympic Games – over that period.

Volkswagen and brand Germany

Volkswagen is one of the world's most trusted car manufacturers. Its brand is built on its reputation for building reliable, innovative, environmentally-friendly cars. In 2015 information came to light from the United States that VW technicians had designed 'cheating' devices into its diesel engines. The devices detected when the cars were being tested for emissions, and adjusted engine performance to temporarily reduce emissions to pass the test. When the cars drive out of the testing station, certain gas emissions are up to 40 per cent higher. The devices were fitted to around 11 million cars worldwide.

As a result of violations of US environmental laws, VW recognized a €6.7 billion provision for 'legal risks', and a further €7.5 billion for 'service measures and recalls' in its 2015 annual financial statement. For a brand that is based on reliability and performance, the effect on its reputation, and the knock-on effect on the trust in German engineering, could be catastrophic. In 2016 the Norwegian sovereign wealth fund (the world's largest) announced that it is to sue VW for providing faulty emissions data, and there are sure to be more lawsuits to follow.

Prior to the scandal, the VW brand was valued at $31 billion. In the six months following publication of the scandal, the value was cut to $21 billion (Brand Finance, 2015). At a national level, 'brand Germany' – not helped by Deutsche Bank (€1.2 billion of legal losses) and the Siemens corruption scandal in 2008 – lost $300 billion in the immediate aftermath of the VW scandal.

Legal losses in financial services

You've read already about the average cost of conduct-related legal losses to the financial services sector. The sector is a rich source of legal risk data and it is worth looking at some of the numbers in more depth. Table 1.1 details loss data that results from legal risk, from 10 global banks over three rolling five-year periods, between 2008 and 2014. The figures show that the cost of legal risk-related issues added up to around $40 billion per year between 2010 and 2014.

Table 1.1 Cost of conduct (over a five-year time frame)

2008–2012	£158 billion
2009–2013	£173 billion
2010–2014	£206 billion

SOURCE: CCP Research Foundation

Another source of data – in the form of litigation expenses and legal fees and expenses – is the quarterly financial summaries (form Y-9C) that US bank holding-companies have to complete and file with the Federal Reserve. 'Litigation expenses' are costs associated with litigation and include external legal fees, provisions, awards, etc. The Fed gives no guidance as to what to include within 'Legal fees and expenses' but we take it to mean the external legal spend on non-litigation matters, and it may include the internal cost of the legal function.

We reviewed Y-9C forms for four banks between 2010 and 2014, and charted 'Litigation expenses' and 'Legal fees and expenses' for each bank in Figure 1.1. Our analysis shows that when you exclude litigation expenses, each bank had stable legal fees and expenses over the five-year period; but when litigation expenses are taken into account, the average rise in legal costs over the five-year period was 260 per cent.

Figure 1.1 Litigation and legal expenses

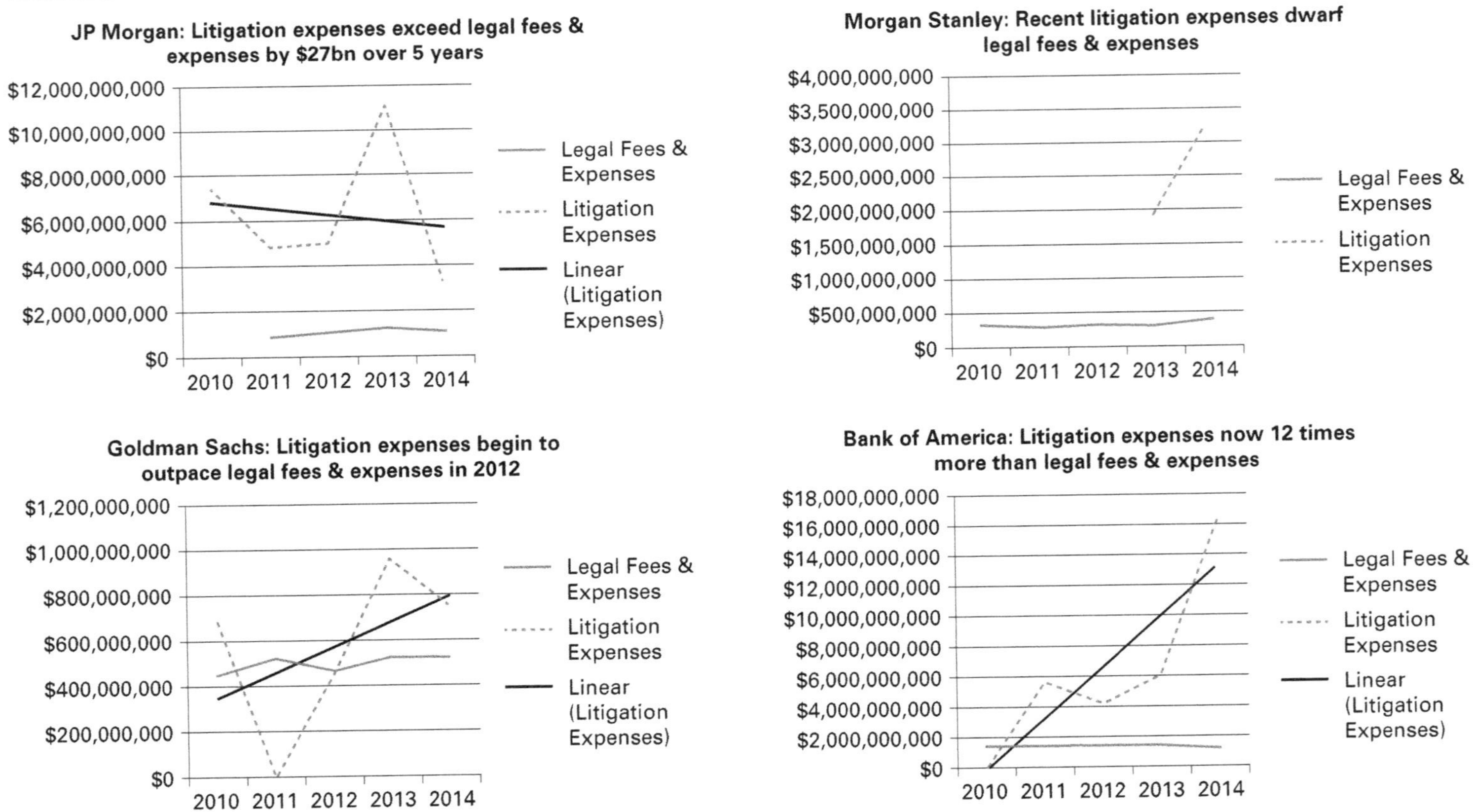

A significant majority of litigation (whether justified or not) is the result of something that you have done as a business. These figures make a good argument that investing in proactive legal risk management to identify where business practices could result in litigation, makes sound business sense. If you focus your company's efforts on changing working practices and reduce the volume and cost of litigation and regulatory investigations you can potentially save huge sums.

Regulator sanctions in the financial services reflect a cultural change in attitude

This sector also gives us data that show how financial services regulator sanctions have increased to a level that is forcing behavioural change. Figure 1.2 shows fines imposed by four regulators across the United Kingdom and United States. The data show clearly the step-change in attitudes towards enforcement since 2012.

> Banks appear to be focusing on issues that are receiving enhanced regulatory attention, rather than proactively considering their own risks relative to the regime as a whole. (FSA, 2012: 74)

Figure 1.2 The step-change in approach from regulators in financial services

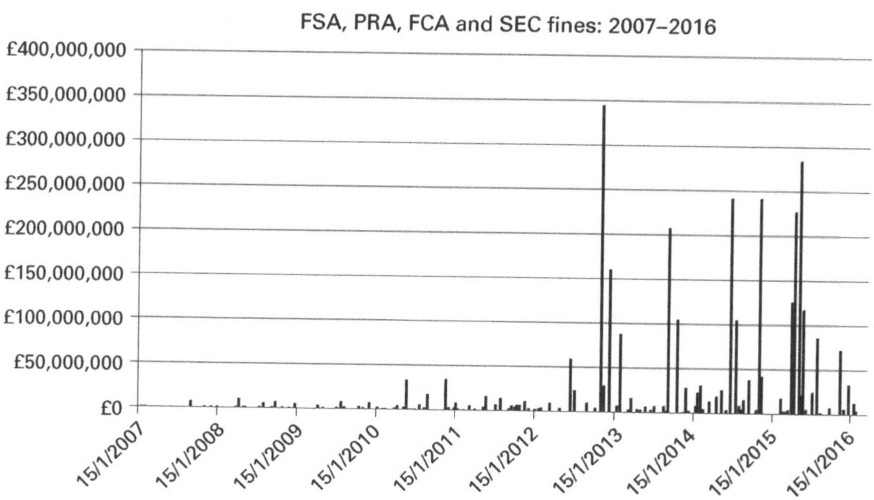

As compelling as this chart is (and you will see it again later in this book), the narrative from regulators tells its own story. In the United States, the SEC is keen to stress its 'record-breaking year'. Andrew Cresney, Director of the SEC's Enforcement Division, said:

> The Division's hard work, tremendous energy, and efficiency uncovered significant misconduct during the past fiscal year, and helped bring a significant number of high-impact, first-of-their-kind actions. I continue to be proud of the Division's record of accomplishments, and we have already continued to pave new ground in the new fiscal year.

These regulators are, of course, reacting to a societal shift that began shortly after the financial crisis in 2008 and that is felt in other sectors. These fines reflect a change in public attitude towards big business that is discussed in more depth in Chapter 5 of this book.

Why you should treat legal risk as part of operational risk

There are different ways to manage legal risk. Some organizations will say that they manage their legal risk by employing good lawyers to negotiate contracts, or by having a panel of approved law firms to turn to when they are being sued or want to bring a case against a third party. Although the outcome of legal risk is often incurred through regulator sanction or litigation, legal risk originates from a broad set of operational interactions between your business practices and the laws and regulations that apply to them. Banking supervisors in particular have embraced the relationship between operating practices and legal risk and are responsible for three significant events that have helped to define the operational context and scope of legal risk:

1. The Basel Committee put legal risk in scope of operational risk, and gave lawyers a new way to view the impact of their profession on business.

2 The International Bar Association Banking Group Working Party created its long-standing definition of legal risk (see Box 1.2 on legal risk definitions towards the end of this chapter) that has served as a starting point for many legal risk identification and management initiatives.

3 The European Banking Authority put ethical conduct in the scope of legal risk, and stated that legal risk losses should be recorded as operational loss.

1. The Basel Committee

The Basel Committee for Banking Supervision (BCBS) is the primary global standard-setter for the prudential regulation of banks. It provides a forum for cooperation on banking supervisory matters. Its mandate is to strengthen the regulation, supervision and practices of banks worldwide with the purpose of enhancing financial stability. The BCBS seeks to achieve its mandate by sharing information relating to risks and supervisory issues in the banking sector; setting, promoting and monitoring global standards for the regulation and supervision of banks; and sharing information with other bodies interested in promoting financial stability.

In 2003 Pillar 2 of the Basel II Accord stated that (emphasis added): 'Operational risk is the risk of losses resulting from inadequate or failed internal processes, people or systems, or from external events. *It includes legal, but not reputational or strategy risk.*' The exclusion of reputational risk from operational risk is sensible, and aligns with our own perspective. Reputational damage is an outcome of many forms of risk, as is financial loss. Strategy risk – the risks that result from poor business strategy – is similarly not operational in nature. Basel II also defines legal risk in a footnote (see Box 1.2).

2. The IBA

Around the same time as Basel II put legal risk within the lexicon of operational risk, a Banking Group Working party set up by the International Bar Association was tasked with defining legal risk.

The working party, chaired by Roger McCormick who now runs the Conduct Cost Project, drafted the most well-known and widely accepted definition in use today. The definition, which is fundamentally operational in nature, is included in Box 1.2.

3. The European Banking Authority

The most recent developments, and perhaps the most significant, originate in mainland Europe with the European Banking Authority (EBA). The EBA is an independent EU Authority that works to ensure effective and consistent prudential regulation and supervision across the European banking sector. Its overall objectives are to maintain financial stability in the EU and to safeguard the integrity, efficiency and orderly functioning of the banking sector.

The EBA in June 2015 provided final guidance on which types of operational risk loss should be recorded as legal risk. In particular, it includes losses related to (un)'ethical conduct' in scope of legal risk, and excludes the 'risk of being sued' as a risk outcome. Its guidance on which losses should be registered as legal risk losses (see Box 1.1) means that businesses can begin to align legal risk reporting with other forms of operational risk. However, recording loss after the event is a poor way to manage legal risk and is no substitute for early identification of legal risks by your legal teams.

Box 1.1

The EBA list three types of operational loss you should record as a result of legal risk:

1. Legal settlements, either judicial or out of court, such as arbitration, or claims' negotiations.
2. Customer refunds or discounts of future services offered to customers voluntarily in response to or to avoid future legal risk (including offered to customers due to same operational risk event).
3. Losses due to errors and omissions in contracts and documentation.

Three reasons legal risk management is still a niche discipline

Although many businesses rely on lawyers to identify and manage legal risk, it seems that legal risk management doesn't come naturally to them. Lawyers are by training reactive and manage risk situations after the risk event has happened. Law firms have little incentive to help their clients avoid the issues that result in huge fees for them, and in-house teams have failed to make the case to their law firms and to their business that there is a difference between 'good' and 'bad' legal spend. Bad legal spend is money spent managing the legal crisis that ensues after an issue has already happened; good legal spend is money spent preventing that issue from happening in the first place. If the legal profession is to play its part in resolving one of the biggest risk issues to face business today, educators, private practice and in-house lawyers need to change the way they perceive legal risk in business.

1. Legal education is geared towards dispute protection

This is perhaps a sweeping generalization, but although traditional legal education does teach lawyers a degree of risk management, it emphasizes risk management towards the potential of a court dispute, or as an ambiguity within the scope of the law itself. There are courses that look at the law in context and, for example, at the importance and impact of regulators, but there are few that focus on proactive legal risk management as we define it in this book and as it is applied in business. There have been some efforts to change this, for example through teaching the work in the 1950s of US attorney Louis Brown. Brown wrote about preventive law and urged his colleagues to deliver legal 'health checks' to their clients. He was responsible for some significant improvements in the way law was taught, but these are unfortunately isolated examples in a profession that still focuses on how to win future lawsuits rather than how to prevent lawsuits from happening. There is still a long journey ahead for the legal education system to move towards a more holistic, operational view of legal risk.

You will find many examples of this disconnect between legal training and commercial reality. The International Association for the Commercial and Contract Management (IACCM) conducts annual research that compares the most negotiated contract terms with the terms that are most important to success of the supplier-customer relationship. In the 2013/14 survey only five of the top 10 most negotiated terms matched the list of top 10 terms that were most important to the success of the relationship (see www2.iaccm.com, 2016). The report is optimistic that this improves on the results of previous years – in past surveys around 80 per cent of respondents acknowledged that their negotiation focus didn't bring about the best result for either party – but there is still a clear gap between what lawyers are taught to focus on in contract negotiations and what matters commercially.

2. Private practice cares only about the transaction

Law firms earn significant fees from clients that are in crisis. Lawyers deliver an undoubtedly valuable service when you are in trouble, or when you need a legal structure to wrap around your business's deals. But private practice law hasn't yet accepted that there is value in offering proactive advice to clients that will help them avoid future issues. The focus is on how to win the next lawsuit, not how to prevent it.

There are of course exceptions and hopefully more will emerge, but the big litigation practices that have the best insights into how your business can avoid legal risk (they see how businesses get it wrong time and again) have far more to gain from advising clients in crisis than advising clients how to prevent them. Also it is surprisingly difficult for even those practices that want to give that type of advice to do so. Senior partners in firms are quite open that it is more difficult to persuade a client to spend $20,000 fixing its contracts to prevent a dispute, than to spend $2 million to defend a commercial litigation. 'Bad spend' seems to win out over 'good spend' every time.

3. In-house legal teams are in the eye of the perfect storm

For the in-house counsel, at the front-line of legal risk in business, the world has changed fundamentally since 2006. If you are a General Counsel, you will be under pressure (possibly for the first time) to manage annual budgets and you will have extra responsibilities to manage external legal spend. The increase in transactional and regulatory work means that you have more legal issues to deal with than ever. And if you aren't able to transform your approach to deliver proactive legal risk insights to your business, to help management make better business decisions to avoid legal issues, you run the risk of being marginalized in favour of compliance and regulatory affairs teams.

Because the form of legal loss is often incurred through regulatory sanction, teams that are familiar with working with regulators have become increasingly relevant to business today. These teams are specialists in helping businesses to comply with the letter of regulation, and so have an important role in legal risk management. However, they don't necessarily have the skills to identify changes in the law that drive regulatory attitudes, and they almost certainly won't have the skills to identify and manage other legal risks that can result in legal loss, such as contractual failings or failures in duty of care, or to advise on areas such as intellectual property and the impact of digitalization, where you can gain business advantage by staying ahead of the curve.

In-house lawyers have much work to do if they are to create better outcomes for business, but there are potentially great advantages. When in-house legal teams adapt operational risk tools to manage legal risk, they develop the ability to assess business interactions with the law for potential risks and deliver great risk management outcomes and real business advantage. Later in this book you will learn what a good, operational-risk based, legal risk management framework looks like, and how to apply it in your own business operations. The foundation of any risk management framework is the ability to articulate clearly the risk that you are trying to prevent.

How legal risk has been defined since 2000

So the starting point for lawyers and operational risk managers is to find a way to articulate legal risk clearly, in a way that identifies the originating root interactions between law and regulation and your business. Because the outcome of many risks is often 'legal', for example regulator sanction or litigation, it is important to keep in mind the distinction between what is a legal risk 'origin' and what is a legal 'outcome'.

There are two basic principles you can apply that lead to a clear scope and articulation of legal risk. First, the law in itself is not a risk. The law exists to protect the stakeholder. It can change, and you must be able to adapt to that change, but you should focus the scope of your definition on the way your business interacts with law and regulation and in particular the key interactions where there is potential for individuals to make decisions or take action that could fall outside the letter or spirit of the law. Second, use legal language to define legal risk. If lawyers are to have responsibility for identifying legal risk, it should be defined in language that is at its core legal in nature. That doesn't mean it has to be confusing and without punctuation! It means language that tacks the operational practice back to its originating root interaction with the law. From our practical experience, any non-legal term will be used at some point to dispute ownership of legal risk management controls.

Box 1.2 details the different ways that legal risk has been defined since 2000. This is useful background on how others have approached legal risk, but in the final section of this chapter we will explain how to apply these two fundamental principles to build a robust definition of legal risk for your own business, and how we have used them to create our own definition.

Box 1.2 History of legal risk definitions

2000: Bank of England (oversight of payment systems)

In 2000, the Bank of England had oversight of the UK's payment systems. The payment systems transferred money equivalent to around half of UK GDP every day. They were and are of worldwide systemic importance.

In its oversight paper the Bank of England (2000) gave some background on payment systems in the United Kingdom and the risks involved. Of particular interest is paragraph 42, which sets out how the Bank proposed to report on 'the risk that unexpected interpretation of the law or legal uncertainty will leave the payment system or members with unforeseen financial exposures and possible losses'. Its approach introduces the concept of uncertainty with regards to the law itself, and articulates financial loss as the outcome to avoid.

2001: Financial Law Panel

The Financial Law Panel took a different and much more detailed approach in 2001, and gave useful examples of how it envisaged legal risks being realized. Legal risk situations affecting the company may be grouped under three headings:

1 *Organizational legal risk:* the risk connected with the maintenance of the company's assets and property and with internal affairs of the company. Examples:

   - Risk that the company might fail adequately to protect its intellectual property assets or that the ownership and/or value of these assets might be successfully challenged by third parties.
   - Risk of liability to shareholders or that shareholders might be able to compel action contrary to the wishes of management.
   - Risk that management action may fail to take proper account of employment law or of the rights of employees or trade unions.
   - Possibility that the company may fail to see the consequences of an act or omission because of: a) failure to take appropriate legal advice; b) shortage or inadequacy of in-house legal advice; or c) defects in internal procedures for identifying when legal advice is needed.

▶

2 *Legal methodology risk:* risk that the methods adopted and steps taken to protect the company's assets against claims by others or to protect against liability to pay damages or compensation to others are inadequate. Examples:

- In a commercial transaction, the company does not take warranties from its counterparty, but relies instead on its due diligence procedures. The due diligence fails to reveal a defect, leaving the company with no legal recourse.
- The use of standard or 'generic' legal opinions on the content of legal rules in overseas jurisdictions may fail to reveal an issue relevant to a particular transaction because of the general nature of the opinion given.
- Risk that the only available method of taking protection can never be completely effective. For example, opinions given about the ownership of and capacity of 'tax haven' companies with bearer shares can never in practice avoid the possibility of fraud.

3 *Conduct of business legal risk:* risk that, in the course of the conduct of the company's operations, it will incur obligations or liabilities that were not foreseen or are greater than were foreseen, or that its rights and claims prove to be fewer or of a lower value than had been expected. Examples:

- The possibility that contractual rights will be void or unenforceable because of illegality, technical defect or lack of capacity of either party.
- The possibility that contractual or statutory provisions may be interpreted differently by a court than by the company.
- The possibility that the court will take a different view on a technical point from that on which the company has relied.
- The possibility that legal proceedings will have an adverse consequence greater than expected (or a favourable consequence lower than expected) eg the company takes a more optimistic view of the outcome of litigation or regulatory proceedings.
- The operations of the company produce unforeseen liabilities to third parties.
- The possibility that the company's operations might infringe the legal rights of third parties.

- Risk that the company's claims will not be capable of satisfaction in practice (eg due to insolvency of the judgement debtor).
- Difficulty of enforcing legal rights on other jurisdictions with which the company is less familiar.

2003: International Bar Association – Banking Law Committee working group

The IBA definition is perhaps the best known of all the definitions published in the last 10 years. It is distinctly operational in nature.

Risk of loss to an institution which is primarily caused by:

a a defective transaction; or

b a claim being made or some other event occurring which results in a liability for the institution or other loss (for example, as a result of the termination of a contract); or

c failing to take appropriate measures to protect assets (for example intellectual property) owned by the institution; or

d change in law.

The IBA definition includes extensive notes on interpretation, which we haven't included here.

2003: Financial Services Authority

The Financial Services Authority (FSA) was the United Kingdom's sole financial regulator for 10 years up to 2013. At its inception, the FSA brought together the previous regulatory material on prudential requirements that applied to insurers, banks and other firms carrying on financial services. It created a separate interim Prudential Sourcebook for each of the main financial sectors, with the intention of eventually consolidating prudential guidance for all sectors into a single integrated Prudential Sourcebook. The interim sourcebook for insurers, which is referred to as IPRU (INS), contained a now deleted guidance note that defined legal risk as follows:

Risk that the law is proved to operate in a way adverse to the interests or objectives of the insurer where the insurer:

- *did not consider its effect;*
- *believed its effect to be different; or*
- *operated with uncertainty as to its effect.*

▶

This is similar to the approach the Bank of England took in 2000, and introduced the concept that adverse effects could arise through uncertainty in the way that people understand the law.

2004: Basel Committee

The Basel Committee is the primary global standard-setter for the prudential regulation of banks and provides a forum for cooperation on banking supervisory matters. Its mandate is to strengthen the regulation, supervision and practices of banks worldwide with the purpose of enhancing financial stability. In a footnote to its definition of operational risk, the Basel Accord defined legal risk as follows: 'Legal risk includes, but is not limited to, exposure to fines, penalties, or punitive damages resulting from supervisory actions, as well as private settlements.' This is deliberately non-exclusive in nature, but introduces more detail on the types of loss to be included – fines, penalties or punitive damages – and has as its scope commercial and regulatory disputes.

2004: International Association of Insurance Supervisors

Established in 1994, the IAIS represents insurance regulators and supervisors of more than 200 jurisdictions in nearly 140 countries, constituting 97 per cent of the world's insurance premiums. Its objectives are to promote effective and globally consistent supervision of the insurance industry in order to develop and maintain fair, safe and stable insurance markets for the benefit and protection of policyholders, and to contribute to global financial stability.

In 2004 it issued a Guidance Paper on Anti-money Laundering and Combating the Financing of Terrorism. That contained a footnote definition of legal risk: 'Legal risk: the possibility that lawsuits, adverse judgements or contracts that turn out to be unenforceable disrupt or adversely affect the operations or condition of an insurer' (see http://iaisweb.org/index.cfm?event=getPage&nodeId=25237).

2004: International Institute for the Unification of Private Law (UNIDROIT)

In his paper on legal risk and market efficiency, Guy Morton defined legal risk in terms of legal uncertainty: 'The risk that the law fails to deliver predictable and practical result' (see http://www.unidroit.org/english/documents/2004/study78/s-78-012-e.pdf).

This kind of risk may arise in a number of ways. A law may be uncertain, widely misunderstood or not clearly defined, or a law may be very clear and well understood but simply not up to the task. It may be defective; it may be incomplete; it may leave gaps that simply do not permit people to do the transactions they would like to do, or it may be burdensome; it may impose irrelevant antiquated or over-engineered procedural requirements that make it expensive and cumbersome to operate.

2015: European Banking Authority

The next 'official' definition wasn't seen until 2014, when the EBA published its consultation paper on technical standards for an Advance Model Approach to capital models. Although the draft paper did contain a definition of legal risk, the final version, published in 2015, steered clear of providing a formal definition of legal risk. This is an important and current paper, so we have derived a definition by piecing together the different elements of it that refer to the consequence or cause of legal loss:

> *Legal risk can be defined as operational risk events and losses that are triggered by a breach of obligations for the institution that derive from statutory or legislative provisions, of national or international origin, or from contractual arrangements, or internal rules and ethical conduct that derive from national or international norms and practices.*
> *(From EBA final draft RTS on AMA assessment for operational risk; https://www.eba.europa.eu/-/eba-publishes-final-draft-standards-on-assessment-methodologies-to-use-advanced-measurement-approaches-for-operational-risk)*

It is important to note that both accidental and deliberate or negligent (misconduct) breaches are considered to be in the scope of legal risk, as is 'ethical conduct'.

Our legal risk definition and short-form legal risk taxonomy

You articulate legal risk through the means of a legal risk definition. Box 1.2 shows how this has been done in the past, typically by grouping together some examples of how legal risk could originate (for example 'breach of obligations'), with some examples of legal outcomes (for example risk of being sued), and badging the group collectively as 'legal risk'. Our own definition and taxonomy will enable you to differentiate between origination and outcome, and will result in clear and meaningful operational implementation of preventative measures. We created our own definition and taxonomy by following these five steps, and have applied both to real-life projects in multiple sectors:

> From an operational perspective it is easy to mistake responsibilities for legal risk identification with responsibilities for legal risk ownership. There is a clear difference between the responsibility to identify the legal consequences of an action, and the responsibility for the action itself.

Step 1. Articulate the form of loss you want to prevent

There are two forms of loss that your legal risk management programme should try to prevent: direct financial loss (for example large fines or regular contract leakage) and indirect reputational loss (that can affect brand value and potentially the long-term sustainability of your business).

Step 2. Explain in abstract form the action that could lead to the loss event

To bring the definition to life and give a hook for operational implementation, you need to articulate the human behaviour that can lead to the loss. When people in your business interact with law and regulation there are three possible behaviours that can lead to loss: misunderstanding of the way the law applies, ambiguity in the law, or the rogue, 'reckless indifference' to the fact that law may apply.

Step 3. Clarify the scope for your legal risk management activities

Clearly stating the scope helps to give a boundary for legal risk management activities. If you are looking at legal risk for business, for example, you would state the scope as your 'business, its relationships, processes, products and services'. This is also the first step in the ISO 31000 risk management process that is part of the foundation for our own legal risk management framework.

When you join steps 1, 2 and 3 together you create a good policy-level definition that explains succinctly what legal risk is and how it arises:

> *Legal risk is the risk of financial or reputational loss that can result from lack of awareness or misunderstanding of, ambiguity in, or reckless indifference to, the way law and regulation apply to your business, its relationships, processes, products and services.*

Step 4. Prescribe high-level categories of interaction

A succinct policy-level definition is a great start, but to implement the definition at an operational level and to capture the bottom-up activity from your operating practices you need to refine the scope further. Focus legal risk management on the specific ways that law and regulation interact with your business and create a typology or taxonomy of legal risk. To be an effective tool that will guide your efforts to identify legal risk, your taxonomy must be *collectively exhaustive:* be able to house any and all legal risk from your business; and *mutually exclusive:* house each legal risk in a single category. 'Anything less is little more than a collection of useful examples' (Mahler, 2007).

We've established five key originating categories of legal risk from past definitions and our own work of the last 10 years in identifying legal risk for our clients:

1 *Legislative regulatory risk:* the risk that you fail to adequately implement and comply with law and regulation. There is an argument that all legal risk could be put into this category, but that is flawed. Failing to comply with law and regulation is a risk in itself, and many people are employed in compliance functions to manage just that risk. But there are many other ways that legal risk can result in financial and reputational loss outside of the legislative/regulatory framework.

2 *Non-contractual obligations risk:* essentially the risk that the business fails to meet its duty of care to customers, the environment, its stakeholders and the market. This category is the most fluid, as duty of care (or obligations under tort) is woolly, tricky to define and inconsistently applied in the courts. This category is prioritized through the courts and the enforcement actions of regulators, and gives rise to the risk of potential criminalization of individuals in positions of responsibility within the company. In civil law jurisdictions these risks are covered by the concept of 'civil duty'.

3 *Contractual risk:* the risks that your current – and future – contracts expose you to. This is usually the biggest source of regular loss. Risk management activities should be split between ensuring that the terms are fair and enforceable, the agreement is commercially viable and that the business use contracts in the right way at the right time.

4 *Dispute risk:* we deliberately limit the scope of dispute risk to the actions that you take within the bounds of the dispute itself. The root cause of dispute is either mismanagement of another type of risk (contractual disputes, for example) or a speculative claim from a third party. So the risks you can actually manage within this category, and that affect your quantum of loss, relate to the operational or strategic decisions you take from the moment you become aware that a dispute is a potential outcome.

5 *Non-contractual rights risk:* from a practical perspective non-contractual rights boil down to IP-related risks. You could fail to register your own rights, or fail to enforce against infringement of others. Some of your biggest business risks could result from potential failures to identify, protect and leverage your IP to take advantage of the effects of digitalization on your sector.

Step 5. Create your taxonomy, flesh out each risk category with a comprehensive set of descriptive examples

The final step is to flesh out your high-level legal risk categories with a more detailed second level. These second level categories give you a good degree of granularity in your data so that you can create meaningful reports that speak to which specific practices can lead to legal risk.

To create the second level, draw a map of your business process from end to end, work through where that process interacts with law and regulation, and write down the risks that could lead to misunderstanding, lack of knowledge or deliberate, careless or reckless indifference to the law. To shortcut the process, we've fleshed out each of the five categories above with a set of descriptive examples that, we believe, represent a mutually exclusive and collectively exhaustive group. If you read through the lists and have questions about whether a particular example from your own business should be classed as contractual, or legislative – think through which is the originating factor and choose that one. Table 1.2 sets out a robust two-level legal risk taxonomy you can apply to any business. Throughout this book you will read how to use this tool with standard operational risk management techniques to identify and manage legal risks in your business.

Table 1.2 Our short-form legal risk taxonomy

Legislative/regulatory risk	Failure to adequately comply, failure to assess, failure to monitor changes
Non-contractual obligations risk	Unintentional assumption of duty of care, failure in duty of care to customers, markets, environment or staff
Contractual risk	Failure to enter into a binding agreement, unintentional waiver or amendment to contract, unintended consequences from amendment or waiver to contract, failure to use standard terms, inadequate or unclear terms, unfair terms or unenforceable terms, lack of awareness of terms
Dispute risk	Failure to protect privilege, inappropriate resolution regime, failure to adhere to dispute timeline
Non-contractual rights risk	Failure to protect, failure to enforce against infringement

Summary

We hope that in reading this chapter you've gained a clear understanding of how legal risk can affect your business. The examples of direct financial loss can be applied to any sector: although it may seem that the financial services sector has suffered more than most, its pain is not unique. The direct losses and reputational damage to household names such as VW or Petrobras have had a knock-on effect on other national businesses and even the national brand value. The combined effects of Siemens, Deutsche Bank and VW, for example, knocked an estimated $300 billion off the German national brand!

Putting together a business case for legal risk management requires more than scaremongering, relaying stories of eye-watering loss and career-threatening headlines. You need to appreciate the overlap with other risk areas, in particular with operational risk, and the role that the in-house legal team has to play in identifying and managing legal risk. When you define legal risk through discreet categories, as we have done here, which map operational activity to potential legal loss, you begin to create a framework that enables you to pinpoint legal risk in your business and apply operational risk management techniques to manage it. In a world where the legal and regulatory environment is so complex, and regulatory enforcement so aggressive, businesses that learn to navigate this legal landscape cost-effectively can gain real competitive advantage.

Big picture legal risk management 02

Corporate governance, values and policy

We've begun to look at governance – at the systems that improve quality – and realize there's a dichotomy between the values set out in policy, and how they are enacted in process. (Graham Copnell)

Introduction

Our legal risk definition and taxonomy set out in Chapter 1 form the foundation of much of the rest of this book. You will read how to apply it in practice to quantify legal risk and to report clearly your exposure. You will also read in detail how the five key interactions between your business and law/regulation can be managed to protect your business from legal loss.

Before we get engrossed in detailed legal risk management frameworks and techniques, let's step back and look at how legal risk is traditionally managed by your board. The decisions you take at board level set the parameters within which legal risk must be managed. No sane CEO would set out a business strategy that could result in huge losses and possible criminal sanction, and no sensible board would rubber-stamp decisions that could potentially ruin the business. At a macro level, organizations have set out corporate governance structures, value statements and policies to guide their businesses in how to operate within the bounds of law and regulation.

But the corporate governance structures that boards put in place to ensure their decisions are implemented have come under increasing scrutiny since the financial crisis. There is a rising tide of regulatory reform aimed, in part, at strengthening corporate accountability that demands prudent institutions reassess the effectiveness of their existing corporate governance structures. You are increasingly being required to evidence how corporate governance principles are applied not just at board level, but throughout your organization wherever management decisions are made.

Post-crisis in the United Kingdom, the Government reviewed the role possible failures in corporate governance could have played in the financial crisis. Traditional 'top-down' corporate governance methods proved to be inconsistent in protecting banks during the crisis. Although banks with effective boards and robust corporate governance tended to survive relatively intact, banks with apparently similar corporate governance frameworks, similar balance sheets, and similar business lines suffered the indignity of a government bail-out, forced restructuring and sustained regulatory supervision. The output of these government reviews, together with similar activity across other jurisdictions, has played a significant role in influencing regulators on both sides of the Atlantic to instil new levels of individual accountability at senior levels in financial services and in particular to reduce the influence of short-termism on corporate action. These changes aim to instil a new ethical perspective to corporate action, and incentivize businesses to follow long-term, sustainable paths to growth.

Change like this doesn't happen overnight. You need to manage it and measure its success within your own organization. If your staff aren't clear where the line is between what is ethical and what is not, their decisions will at some point put you on the wrong side of law and regulation. If your board and senior management don't take seriously their responsibility to oversee the culture and behaviour of people in your business, legal losses are almost certain to follow. This chapter discusses corporate governance and corporate values as a tool to manage legal risk. Great companies implement great corporate governance that has a real influence on front-line behaviour. Lessons from sector-specific reviews post-financial crisis in the

United Kingdom, and developments in health policy in the United Kingdom, provide the perfect foundation to evaluate your own corporate governance framework and its effect on working practices within your organization.

Emerging best practice in corporate governance

Financial services has seen a dramatic shift in corporate governance practices since the financial crisis in 2008. Corporate governance rules are applied differently in different jurisdictions: for instance, the 'comply or explain' approach in the United Kingdom is very different to the US regime of strict compliance, where for example SOX requirements (see below) are mandated by law. Pre-crisis the UK and US regimes had the same aim: they were structural requirements designed to protect the market from fraud and investors from reckless and maverick management. Post-crisis, there has been a significant shift towards how decisions are actually made, how effectively board and corporate culture act as a check and balance to dominant individuals in the boardroom, and how effectively they influence culture and behaviour throughout the business.

Sarbanes-Oxley (SOX)

The Sarbanes-Oxley bill was enacted in the United States as a reaction to a number of major corporate and accounting scandals, including Enron and WorldCom. It contains 11 sections covering auditor independence, boardroom failures, banking practices and executive compensation. It required the Securities and Exchange Commission (SEC) to create regulations to define how public corporations are to comply with the law.

As a result of SOX, top management must individually certify the accuracy of financial information. Penalties for fraudulent financial activity are much more severe. SOX increased the oversight role of boards of directors and the independence of the outside auditors who review the accuracy of corporate financial statements.

The adoption of new best practice in corporate governance has spread throughout other jurisdictions. There are instances where group parent companies, in emerging and developing markets where corporate governance practices are still evolving, look to the United Kingdom as the standard for corporate governance best practice in order to form their own framework. As these non-UK group parent companies become more familiar with UK (and, as applicable, local) practices they also increasingly undertake independent corporate governance audits in addition to any conducted by the firm's internal auditors. These independent audits further strengthen corporate governance throughout the group. They incentivize management to continue to prioritize corporate governance and to consider how it is best applied and evidenced. They also promote a more international understanding of corporate governance and possible consolidation and reinforcement of international principles and approaches.

We've distilled the essence of emerging best practice in corporate governance into three broad lessons that we will detail in the rest of this chapter:

1. *Implement value-based corporate governance.* To ensure that all staff throughout your organization are aware of the impact of their individual behaviour on your business, you must clearly articulate your business values and, in particular, how you will maintain a balance between delivering value for customers, robust financial performance, and maintaining good relationships with the market.
2. *Get the basics in place in the boardroom.* It is a growing trend across the world to set out basic standards of corporate governance with which businesses of all sizes must comply. At a minimum, you must comply with these basic standards and ensure that your boardroom is a place where healthy challenge and debate are encouraged, and where directors have responsibilities to ensure your company goals are achieved within a value framework that matches legal and regulatory expectations and that will stand up to increased regulatory scrutiny.
3. *Measure the impact of your corporate governance.* You cannot simply assume that because you have a great corporate value statement and clearly drafted corporate policies, your business will

operate as you have said it should. You need to measure and evaluate the impact of your board structure, your value statement and your corporate policies on the myriad individual decisions that your business takes every day, and take steps to change working practices if you find they don't support your corporate values.

The move towards value-based corporate governance

Because the risks your business takes are usually known and considered at board level, a large part of corporate governance is designed to ensure those decisions are taken to the best of the board's collective ability. The way those decisions are implemented into operational practices is also now the subject of regulatory scrutiny and, where the practices could potentially breach the letter or spirit of the law, a source of legal risk. Post-crisis, evaluation of effective corporate governance has moved beyond compliance with a set of guidelines and towards measuring the influence of the board on corporate culture and conduct. The focus on duty – as a moral commitment to either customers, the market, your stakeholders (staff, investors, etc) or the environment – has brought a new focus on 'corporate ethics' and you need to have robust methods in place to check that your corporate values are enacted in the right way throughout your organization.

The drive to move away from short-term thinking

The widespread move towards value-based governance systems began in the aftermath of the financial crisis. The short-termism that was prevalent in the markets pre-2008 is seen as a key driver behind the behaviours that led to the crash. In the main, large corporations and in particular large financial institutions had got themselves into a situation where the long-term lack of individual accountability – afforded by the corporate legal structure – resulted in corporate cultures that focused on what was right for the corporation, or the individuals running it, rather than the value the corporation delivered to its customers and to society. Corporate governance broke down, with dramatic results.

Two Government reviews in the United Kingdom, the Walker Review in 2009 and the Kay Review in 2012, set out to explore how this could happen. They delivered a set of recommendations to improve governance within banks and within the market as a whole. Key to those recommendations is the thought that messages set at the top of the corporation need to be enacted at the bottom. There needs to be a clear link between what is said to be happening and what happens in reality.

The Walker Review

> Improvement in corporate governance will require behavioural change in an array of closely related areas in which prescribed standards and processes play a necessary but insufficient part. (Walker, 2009)

In February 2009, in light of the financial crisis, the UK Government commissioned a review of corporate governance in UK banks. The committee recommended substantial changes to the way the boards of banks and big financial institutions function. In total the report made 43 recommendations to improve corporate governance in banks, including five on the governance of risk. It didn't limit itself to governance within the corporation: as well as the recommendations on corporate governance within the company, the Walker review recommended implementation of a Stewardship Code, to guide the behaviour of institutional investors. The Stewardship Code was also included in the Kay Review in 2012, which investigated the effect of short-termism on UK equity markets.

Terms of reference of the Walker Review, 2009

To examine corporate governance in the UK banking industry and make recommendations, including in the following areas: the effectiveness of risk management at board level, including the incentives in remuneration policy to manage risk effectively; the balance of skills, experience and independence required on the boards of UK banking institutions; the effectiveness of board practices and the performance of audit, risk, remuneration and nomination committees; the role of institutional shareholders in engaging effectively with companies and monitoring of boards; and whether the UK approach is consistent with international practice and how national and international best practice can be promulgated.

The Kay Review

In 2011, two years after the Walker Review was published, the UK Government commissioned a further review to investigate short-termism in the UK markets (BIS, 2011). It believed that an ineffective equity market would stifle growth of UK business and innovation, and the market focus on short-term performance – driven by the use of shareholder value as a performance metric – would result in unrealistic growth expectations. The expectation that businesses would deliver 10 or 15 per cent growth year on year was found to be to a large extent responsible for the failure in corporate culture, and subsequent decline of trust and misalignment of incentives throughout the equity investment chain.

> **Terms of reference of the Kay Review, 2012**
>
> To examine the mechanisms of corporate control and accountability provided by UK equity markets and their impact on the long-term competitive performance of United Kingdom businesses, and to make recommendations.

> Short-termism is a problem in UK equity markets, and that the principal causes are the decline of trust and the misalignment of incentives throughout the equity investment chain. (Kay, 2012)

The Kay and Walker Reviews have in part led to two significant steps that financial institutions are being required to implement to guard against short-term thinking and instil the 'right' culture. They created a link between executive remuneration and long-term corporate objectives, and in particular want to ensure that large bonuses will be paid back if the objectives they are linked to are proven to be bad for long-term performance. As part of the move away from short-termism, they seek to encourage a corporate culture that keeps financial performance in balance with other objectives, such as delivering quality work, treating customers fairly and building healthy relationships with the market as a whole. In particular, the reviews highlighted the role of the board in setting corporate culture and values.

Corporate governance in the boardroom

The board as your leadership committee sets strategy, decides operational capability, reviews company performance and sets your company's values and standards. A robust board, with a clear sight of your organizational values and how they affect the way you achieve your objectives, is vital to good corporate governance. Failures in corporate governance can lead to direct legal action: the decision by the Norwegian sovereign wealth fund to join class action against VW seems to be taken as a measure to enforce improved governance of that company. Spokesperson Martha Skaar, said of the decision:

> We've had several meetings with company representatives since the incorrect disclosure was known. At this time we see little evidence of governance reform. We expect VW to conform to acceptable corporate governance standards, including an adequate provision of fully independent directors, and commitment to equitable treatment of shareholders. (Sky News, 2016)

The role of the board and directors

To get the basics in place at board level you need the right balance of personalities and to clearly allocate responsibilities between them.

The chair and the senior independent director

Apart from his or her role leading the board, to ensure it is an effective working group taking responsibility for corporate strategy and representing your shareholders in board meetings, history has shown that your chair should be independent – and should have industry experience relevant to the role. During the financial crisis in the United Kingdom, the banks that required rescue each had chair with no prior banking experience.

The senior independent director acts as the chair's confidante and sounding board, supports him or her in taking decisions, and evaluates his or her performance. Together, the chair and senior independent director have a key role as communicators with shareholders and within the board. If relationships ever break down between shareholders, directors and/or the chair, the senior independent director will step in to resolve disputes and maintain stability. In times of crisis, clear and effective communication with regulators, shareholders and the public can help to quickly limit the damage and restore your reputation. At a practical level, getting your facts straight, being truthful and being consistent are three golden rules of crisis management.

Three golden rules of communication in a crisis

1. *Gather the facts.* Do this as quickly and reliably as possible. If you do not know the necessary facts, you need to acknowledge that you are still investigating rather than try to create something false to satisfy the demand for information.
2. *Never lie.* Do not state falsehoods and have to make necessary corrections after the fact. Credibility will suffer. Regulators will want to know what is happening, and often the public will want to know too.
3. *Be consistent.* Executives must communicate with regulators and the public. Usually regulators will need to have much more information than the public, but in no case should the information given to the regulators and the message given to the public be inconsistent.

Get the right balance between non-executive and executive directors

In the United Kingdom, your board should be made up of around 50 per cent non-executive directors (NEDs) with relevant expertise, and 50 per cent executive directors responsible for day-to-day management and delivery of the company's objectives. Executive directors take responsibility to deliver board strategy, from a company-wide perspective, and objectives that are specific to their executive role. The CEO is the most senior director, with executive responsibility to propose and deliver strategy. Several banking failures have been the result of boards where the CEO has been totally dominant and free to operate without being subject to effective challenge.

Your NEDs are responsible for integrity in decision making and consideration of ethics at board level. It is their job to support the chair and executive directors to instil the appropriate culture, values and behaviours in the boardroom and the wider organization. Their most important role is to challenge the decisions of the executive, and to help manage non-contractual obligations risk by viewing the impact of their decisions through a modern ethical lens. We would like to see independent directors have input into, and oversight of, legal risk management activities for this reason. You will read in Chapter 5 how the ethical interpretation of action has shifted, and that breaches in duty of care are a particular priority of both the courts and regulatory enforcement teams. If boards are to stay on top of shifts in the ethical and legal landscape, they must have regular contact – outside the executive body – with their General Counsel or chief legal officer, and receive good quality, relevant management information that supports them in their role to challenge the executive.

Effective challenge is crucial to board decision making

> The most critical need is for an environment in which effective challenge of the executive is expected and achieved in the boardroom before decisions are taken on major risk and strategic issues.
> (Walker, 2009)

The way that boards make decisions came under severe scrutiny post-crisis. Some banks had dominant CEOs with excessive power and control over the members of the board. These CEOs could operate without fear of question or challenge from within their organization. Other banks have instilled a different culture: one of challenge and argument, where voices are often raised and conversations are usually uncomfortable. While not all boards will welcome loud arguments, your board members must be able to question each other's position and come to collective decisions without fear of recrimination. The essential 'challenge' step, shown in Figure 2.1, needs to be recognized unequivocally and clearly embedded in the board.

Figure 2.1 Effective challenge is crucial to good decision making

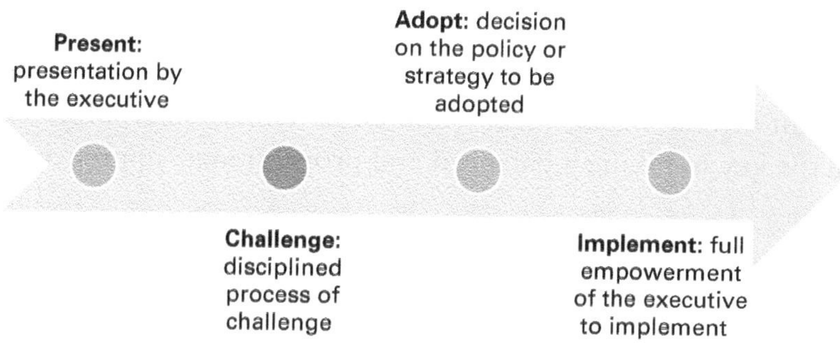

The board and legal risk

The board's role as strategic decision maker puts responsibility for any risks that its business decides to take squarely in its court. Many calamities or crises that affect a company are predictable. They are known to the board in advance and should be managed proportionately. In the pharmaceutical and food industry, for example, many companies' biggest risk is that their products will be kept at the wrong temperature and cause sickness when consumed. If product refrigeration and monitoring weren't priorities at board level, and put at the heart of their operational management strategy, failures could put board members at risk of individual sanction. In finance, IT is an essential foundation for the delivery of financial services, but perhaps not something that was traditionally discussed in great depth at board level. Today, significant failures in banking IT systems will result in regulatory sanction for a failure in duty of care to their customers.

Regulatory compliance is a similar risk in many industries, and the board must take a balanced approach. Many companies refuse to do business in Russia, no matter the potential profitability of the enterprise, because the risk of regulatory violations is simply too high. The local culture of small-scale bribery and large-scale corruption can make it an almost impossible jurisdiction in which they can operate efficiently. By contrast, the same companies are willing to do business in China because while the risk of bribery and corruption is high, the Chinese government has publicly engaged in measures to wipe out such practices: the risk of compliance violations, while existent and known, is seen to be lower and more manageable. The board must be able to view the risks of each jurisdiction in full knowledge of the legal risks. If you have a large and complex business, oversight of risk management – and good management information – are the key to taking a balanced and proportionate approach.

Audit, risk and remuneration committees

Your board retains final responsibility for audit, risk and board remuneration, but it will probably delegate much of the day-to-day work and recommendations to separate committees. Each committee will report regularly to the board and must deliver relevant management information to enable the board to discuss issues and advise the actions of each committee. From a legal risk perspective, for example, executive remuneration has come under particular scrutiny post-crisis as a driver of the sort of short-term thinking that can cause individuals to put profit ahead of value, and breach the letter or spirit of the law in some way. The board and the remuneration committee should ensure that executive remuneration is clearly linked to the company's strategic plan and key performance indicators (KPIs) and focuses on delivery of long-term objectives rather than short-term value.

The annual report

As well as reporting your financial health, your annual report is one of the key ways, together with your annual general meeting (AGM), that you communicate with shareholders and potential investors. It gives you the opportunity to provide a strong narrative on your governance arrangements, strategy, your views on potential risks and what you will do about them. Open and honest narrative in your annual reports can improve your dialogue with shareholders and other stakeholders, and improve their trust and confidence in your business. This narrative is considered to be of such importance in the United Kingdom that requirements for mandatory quarterly reporting have been removed in favour of narrative-rich annual reports. New narratives should avoid 'marketing speak' and should instead give insight into strategy and goals, as well as current financial performance.

Basic corporate governance map

A majority of annual reports contain structure charts similar to that in Figure 2.2. They outline the basic corporate governance structure that you have implemented, and complement the narrative in the report. We have highlighted the company secretary as we see that role developing to take on a broader set of legal risk related responsibilities, and linked each layer of your corporate governance structure to their role in setting, interpreting and enacting your corporate values.

Figure 2.2 Example of a corporate governance map

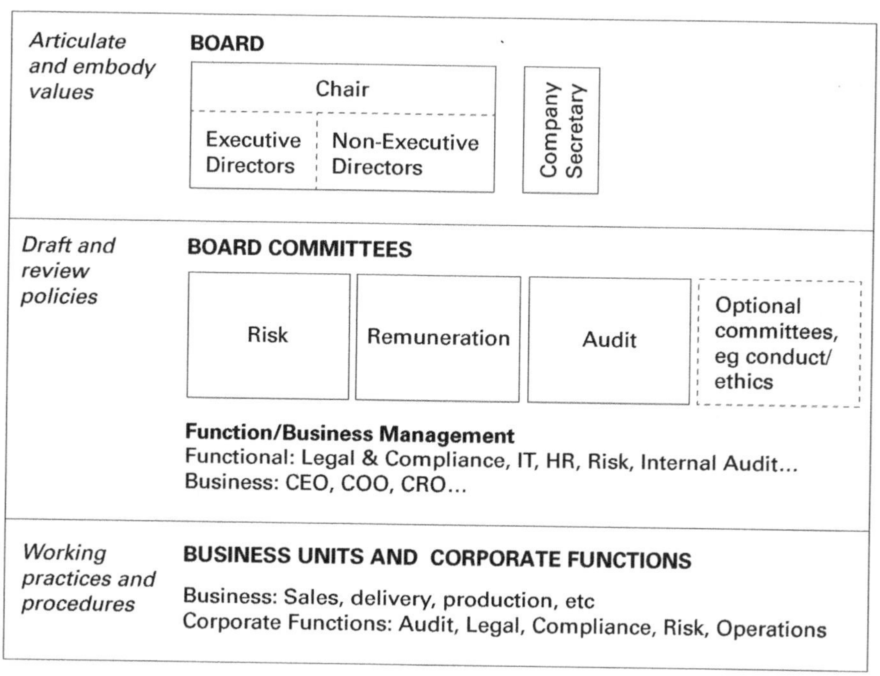

The company secretary

CASE STUDY The evolving role of the company secretary

One key individual who supports the board in implementing corporate governance is the corporate or company secretary. From an implementation perspective, rather than as a matter of liability, the responsibility of ensuring institutions adopt and fully comply with the best practice of corporate governance detailed so far falls increasingly on the company secretarial function. Company secretaries may have traditionally been associated with corporate filings and administrative duties, but partly due to its immediate access to board-level decision making this function often delivers a more hybrid advisory role on potential legal risks at board level. It is common to see job descriptions for company secretarial roles that require a legal background precisely for this reason. The areas where a company secretary can be required to take the lead on corporate governance issues can be varied; below there are some examples of recent trends.

Taken collectively, these developments suggest that the role of a company secretary has changed in the face of increased scrutiny of corporate governance and executive decision making. The role has evolved as boards consider the wide range of regulatory and governance requirements that they need to adhere to and the increasingly prohibitive sanctions for breaching such requirements.

Evaluating the board

Board evaluations are now a crucial tool in testing the performance and governance of the board and it is often the company secretary who is best placed to assess a board's strengths and weaknesses and to offer advice and recommendations as to what can be improved from a procedural perspective as well as to adhere to regulatory and legal requirements. A regular combination of internal and external evaluations ensures that directors, particularly non-executive directors, are less likely to become easily influenced as a result of familiarity and will remain aware of their overriding duty to remain objective, independent and to provide robust challenge. For the chair, the results of an evaluation also provide useful guidance on how proceedings can be altered to comply with developing best practices and requirements. The questions raised and the changes prompted from these external evaluations, together with the discussions they provoke, provide a strong indicator of how important a particular board views the issue of corporate governance and potentially provides an insight into the underlying executive and management culture.

Board remuneration

A particularly sensitive area is the remuneration of executives and directors. Company secretaries are uniquely placed to ensure both the creation and effective operation of remuneration committees and that overall executive remuneration and performance remain within regulatory requirements. While the overall decision on remuneration remains with directors within those frameworks, the company secretary can play a vital role in liaising with independent remuneration consultants and adding independence to the process. Effective corporate governance requires sufficient layers of scrutiny of corporate processes and behaviour, and the company secretarial function provides the first level of internal review and audit.

Conflicts of interest

The issue of conflicts and the potential for conflicts of interest between an institution and its directors is another area which can fall on the company secretary, as well as internal and external legal counsel. Given the access that company secretaries have to the executive and board generally, they are well placed to monitor and document the resolution of issues where there may be a potential conflict. This is increasingly important in jurisdictions such as the United Kingdom where regulators consider the absence of any evidence to show a point was considered and adequately discussed and concluded can itself be construed as a failure of governance.

Board minutes

This ties into the broader responsibility that company secretaries have to accurately minute board meetings and discussions. The emphasis of recent regulatory scrutiny has focused on ensuring that such proceedings are increasingly minuted to show the degree that discussions involve detailed analysis and scrutiny. While company secretaries are only able to minute the actual tone and content of discussions, they are well placed to remind directors of this obligation and to ensure that the presentation of management material to directors enables them to prepare to perform this function.

Lessons in value-based corporate governance

The recommendations in the Walker and Kay Reviews lean heavily towards action over structure. Because action and structure are interconnected, it is of course important to set up the right structures to govern your business, but the actions that they lead to – the behavioural outcomes – are what really matters. Arguably a board's best tool to permanently influence the individual decisions their staff make and avoid costly legal risks is their articulation of corporate values. There are no hard and fast rules for how to articulate value statements, but we can share two very different examples that provide guidance.

The first is an early example of value-based governance that has stood the test of time. Ove Arup was one of the foremost architectural structural engineers of his time. He studied philosophy at Copenhagen University before getting his engineering degree and founding a network of engineering and architectural partnerships that operated under his name 'Arup'. In 1970, with the thought that the founding partners were nearing the end of their careers, Arup wrote and presented his now famous keynote speech, to set out his vision for the future of the partnership.

Ove Arup's speech contains many lessons for modern, value-based corporate governance. He discusses three interconnected goals: quality work, good human relationships, and prosperity for members, shown in Figure 2.3. He urged the future leaders of Arup to keep each of the goals in balance and not to pursue any single goal to the detriment of the others.

Figure 2.3 Arup's three interlocked corporate values

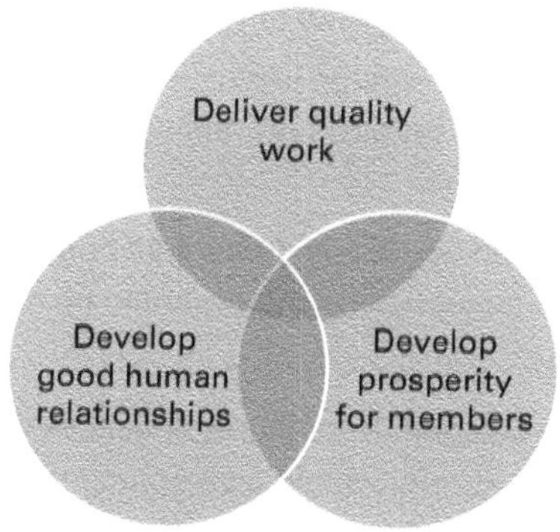

The second example has the brevity of the modern age at heart, but is no less effective in its outcome. Costco is a US wholesale merchandise giant that is wildly successful in supply chain management and is beloved by Costco club members (customers) and employees alike. The mission statement/code of ethics has the following balanced values/objectives:

1 Obey the law.
2 Take care of our members.
3 Take care of our employees.
4 Respect our suppliers.
(Which when managed together will deliver the corporate goal.)
5 Reward our shareholders.

It is worth noting that all of the values have their roots in either the letter or the spirit of the law.

Six lessons in value-based corporate governance

1 Each of your goals is interconnected – the pursuit of individual corporate goals to their full conclusion is done at the expense of other goals. For example, if Arup were to pursue total quality to its natural conclusion with little regard for its customers' actual needs, its relationships would suffer and the pursuit would inevitably lead to reduced prosperity.

2 The pursuit of wealth is important but it isn't everything – the pursuit of wealth is an important prerequisite to the pursuit of your corporate goals, but it is one which, if over-emphasized, can easily get out of hand and become very dangerous for harmony, unity and the company's very existence.
3 Responsibilities should be clearly defined and understood – individual responsibilities for delivering the goals should be defined, understood and accepted by all.
4 Authority should be delegated – authority should be delegated downwards as far as possible. Authority should give good people a reason to stay: why should a good person, who can work anywhere, stay with you?
5 Be flexible in approach – if you are too rigid, your structure can quickly become out of date. Be open to change, and incorporate the lessons that you learn through implementation.
6 Put customers first – your company exists to give value to its customers. Justify the trust they put in you by giving their interest first priority in the work you do for them.

Once you have healthy debate in the boardroom, and a clearly written value statement relevant to your company and designed to encourage your business to achieve a balanced set of goals, you need to evaluate how well each level of your corporate governance structure performs. Does your value statement resonate with your staff? How well is it interpreted into corporate policy? How effective is your policy at influencing the right sort of behaviours and conduct throughout your organization?

How policy works in practice

Earlier in this chapter we said that we would introduce lessons from health policy in the United Kingdom. That sector is important to us because it provides an understanding of how policy works in practice that is directly relevant to working practices across the private sector.

The UK's National Health Service has for many years been an engine of policy. It has separate regulators to cover healthcare quality, finance and standards. It also has separate regulatory bodies for the professional groups that work within the NHS. Just as early efforts to influence corporate culture in the private sector centred solely on setting the right 'tone from the top', for many years the NHS adopted a linear approach to policy development. Policy would be created centrally, communicated to relevant bodies, and implementation would be entrusted to each body with little or no oversight. Unfortunately the NHS has suffered severe incidents that highlight a disconnect between central policy (structure) and individual action. Failures in patient care, coupled with failures to realize intended economic benefits, showed policy makers that the linear model was naïve. They realized that what was said to be done wasn't actually being done in practice. Macro-level policy created at the centre wasn't being implemented at the micro levels through departmental policy and action. This realization led to a focus on governance and management. Policy makers in the healthcare sector began to study how policy worked in practice and they realized that policy is circular.

Figure 2.4 shows both linear and circular policy models and highlights the fundamental differences between their approach to policy. There are three policy levels that translate to the typical business environment. The inner ring represents your board level value statements that set the 'tone from the top'. The middle ring represents your functional and business level policies that interpret the central value statements for specific circumstances. The outer ring represents the myriad individual procedures and practices that evidence how your policies are interpreted and enacted on the shop floor.

Figure 2.4 Linear and circular policy models

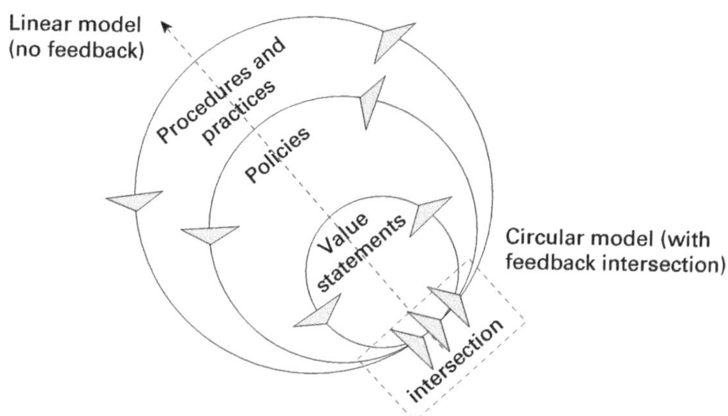

The linear model assumes that actions map straight from boardroom value statements, through policy, to working practices. Because there are insufficient checks, it is quite normal for working practices to develop without reference to the values they are supposed to enact. Because we now know that working practices should feed back into and influence future policy, we appreciate that to implement an effective corporate governance framework we need to focus on the ways that the three policy layers intersect. You need to understand how (and often whether) policy is enacted through effective procedures and what effect the procedures have – in forms of working practices – on the embedded values in your company. If you can gather operational data that show how your policies are interpreted into action, you can assess both how effective your policy framework is in practice and how effective your value statements are at influencing behaviour throughout your organization. This new understanding of how policy works in practice is core to any efforts to evaluate your corporate governance framework.

How to evaluate your corporate governance framework

There is increasing pressure from regulators to make senior individuals directly responsible for failures in corporate governance. If you hold a senior position at a large corporation, you are at significant personal risk. The trend towards criminalization of senior individuals may be necessary to enforce the kind of change in behaviour required in some of our big corporations, but the fuzzy boundaries of the kind of negligence that should be thought of as criminal require the law and its interpretation to be very mature. For example, the extent to which people should be liable for the actions they take at work is debatable: if CEOs were to be held criminally liable for every potential outcome of each and every decision they make for their company, it is difficult to see how they could make any decision at all.

Whether or not the threat of criminal sanction is appropriate, the best defence you have is to ensure you have done everything possible to influence legally and morally acceptable behaviour within your organization. Some people say that the only way to judge the effectiveness of your corporate governance is to see whether you survive the next crisis. When the stakes are so high you cannot afford to be so reactive: you must be proactive and evaluate how effective each element of your governance framework is and how effectively they work together to deliver the right outcomes.

Inside the boardroom there is a structure to evaluate the performance of the chair, the NEDs and the EDs, and the way they interact to make good decisions. Outside of the boardroom, the first step is to look at two of the key elements of governance – your value statement and your policy framework – and the way they interact at a procedural level to create good individual practices. Your value statement, policy framework and individual practices within your organization all have different facets and require different methods of evaluation. In the next section we'll look at each element in turn, and pick out some of the key ways that you can evaluate them.

What to look for in a value statement

Value statements should be concise statements that put individual values such as 'trust', 'respect' and 'fairness' into the corporate context. At a corporate level, you should incorporate somewhere between five and seven values in your overall corporate value statement. Each statement should be brief, but not so brief as to be meaningless. For example, 'Have respect', is too brief, while 'Respect our suppliers' says much more – and is more easily interpretable into corporate policy.

The best value statements resonate throughout the organization. If you want to create a value statement that resonates with your employees, and that your company will continue to work by in 30 years, you must embrace the circularity of policy – and involve your staff in setting those values. There are several ways to do this. We've set out our own six-step guide in the following box.

Involve your staff when you create a new value statement

1. Hold workshops for staff at all levels of the organization. Ask them what values drive them at work – and what values they want to instil at work.
2. Collate unedited output from all the workshops and circulate to the board.
3. Spend a full day with the whole board, to pick out the values that match theirs and that they want to drive forward in the organization.
4. Validate each board-selected value with further staff workshops to check that the board-level interpretation resonates with your staff.
5. Ask some of the key policy holders in your business to read through the value statement and give feedback on how it will influence their current and future actions. If you can evidence that your new values will actually change individual behaviour, you can review whether that behavioural change is in line with your expectations.
6. As a sixth step, you could also hold workshops with customer focus groups, to see how your proposed values might affect their opinion of your brand. Brand interaction is a key driver of business value and this additional step will help avoid unhealthy corporate introspection that could disassociate you from your customer base.

How to evaluate your corporate policies

Corporate compliance is an outflow of legal compliance, so the effectiveness of your internal policies is a key measure of how well you manage legal risk. Your corporate policyholders interpret your value statement into functional and business level policies. They flesh out the values into guidelines that influence individual behaviour within your business. So if your value statement can be interpreted accurately by policyholders into policies that lead to the right behaviours, you will have gone a long way to influencing front-line behaviours in line with your original value statements.

You need to evaluate three facets of each policy:

1. *How well does the policy articulate your values?* Policies articulate values in two ways. They include statements of what you do and do not do; for example you could state that you have 'Zero tolerance for reckless indifference to the law'. They also articulate guidelines of how values should be implemented through working practice.
2. *How well is the policy implemented in practice?* Implementation is measured by what is done, rather than what is said to be done. Check that your written procedures and working practices are a good match to your policies.
3. *How well does the practice reflect the values that policy is trying to deliver?* Because the values that are embedded in policies become diluted in practice, after the policy has been implemented review the procedure and practice against your original value statement and evaluate whether working practices accurately reflect those original values.

The key to good policy is whether the core value is still reflected in the interpretation and action. But few if any corporations test their policies before they are approved. Individuals put a lot of effort into writing policies and they contain many embedded values of the authors. The high degree of author commitment often leads to failures to test its feasibility, and to see whether the policy accurately reflects the core values – and whether it can be implemented in practice. If the policy drives behaviour that demonstrates values you don't intend, then you will need to go back to the drawing (or drafting) board and start again.

Great policies stick to three fundamental principles: simplicity, clarity and communication. Your staff will use policy as a resource to guide their action. They need simple, clear instructions – and to understand how the policy applies to them.

Three top tips for writing great policies

1. *Keep them simple.* The majority of people can hold only three concepts in their mind at one time. Err on the side of caution and try to stick to just one concept per policy.
2. *Write with clarity.* Use short words and an active tense. This will make your policies more readable and therefore more likely to be read.
3. *Tell people which policies apply to them.* You can't hold people to account for failing to apply a policy they aren't aware of and haven't read. You must communicate your policies and take active steps to ensure your people have read and understand them, and know the consequences of failing to follow them.

How to measure the impact of individual actions and behaviours

The decisions your staff make, and the actions they take, expose you to legal risk. There is a constant danger that people in your business will do the wrong thing – whether for the right or wrong reasons – and expose you to potentially significant financial and reputational loss. The tools that most businesses use to measure individual performance are target based; traditionally, little effort is made to check how targets are met. There is evidence that this is changing at a more senior level. The advent of claw-back schemes for executive bonus payments and requirements for board members to invest in company shares are two examples of a concerted effort to move away from short-termism in equity markets. However, there is still a gap in understanding how to map behavioural action at the 'shop floor' to corporate governance frameworks.

Legal risk analysis cuts to the heart of individual decision making. It focuses on the actions your staff take that can result in legal loss. When delivered effectively, as part of a holistic risk management programme, it enables you to quantify the impact of legal risk on your business and measure how effective your working practices are at reducing that exposure. The next chapter will look in detail at how to apply our legal risk taxonomy in practice, to measure the current and future impact of individual actions and behaviours, and identify and quantify legal risks for your own business.

Summary

At a 'big picture' level, the decisions you take in the boardroom set the parameters within which legal risk is managed in your organization. Corporate governance failures were at least partly to blame for banking failures in the financial crisis, in particular where boards were dominated by powerful individuals whose decisions weren't subject to robust challenge. Post-crisis, reviews into corporate governance in the United Kingdom have led to recommendations that companies move away from a checklist-based compliance approach to something akin to a behavioural management tool. Much of the new thinking on corporate governance centres on the make-up of the board, and how to ensure that decisions of CEOs in particular are subject to necessary checks and balances. You also need to be certain that your corporate governance delivers the right behaviours and outcomes outside of the boardroom. Senior executives are at risk of criminal sanction if their organization suffers a severe failure in corporate governance, and this individual accountability has forced boards to take an active interest in how the policy and values they set at board level are interpreted into action throughout their business.

So setting the right tone from the top is now just the starting point. Values are interpreted through policy. If you allow a gap to develop between value and policy or between policy and practice, this will potentially expose you to significant legal risks. At a practical level your core value statement must be simple, relevant and involve people at all levels of the organization. Because the behaviours and day-to-day decisions your staff take expose you to risk every day, you should be proactive and identify where working practices could deviate from legally and morally acceptable norms. This is where a good legal risk framework will help you. It will give you the clear line-of-sight you need at board level to the anomalies and to the individual actions that expose you to potentially significant legal risk.

Evidence you're in control 03

How to identify, quantify and report legal risk

If you see a bump in the road at 50 yards you can do something about it; at five yards you can't.

Introduction

To evidence that your corporation's working practices are in line with your values and don't expose you unnecessarily to legal risk, you need data. You need data that speaks not just to the internal reference point of your corporate value statement and policy framework, but also to the external reference points of law and regulation. You can suffer legal losses not just through fines from regulators and the financial costs related to litigation, but also through the cost of delivering to poor commercial contracts, missed opportunity costs (for example through IP management), failures in contractual controls over credit risk, and the reputational damage associated with all of the above. This chapter is a 'nuts and bolts' guide that will help you to gather meaningful data about which parts of your business carry the biggest exposure to these types of legal loss, the behaviours that could lead to the losses being realized, and what you can do to mitigate the potential exposure.

Legal risk is typically considered to be part of operational risk, and our own framework leans heavily on the best practices from that risk specialism. However, you cannot simply apply an operational risk management framework to identify and quantify legal risk. You need to adapt the framework so that it is meaningful to in-house legal teams and clearly articulates the underlying legal risk. This is where the legal risk taxonomy set out in the first chapter is applied in practice, to identify where your business, its relationships, products and services interact with law and regulation in ways that could lead to financial or reputational loss.

Once you identify your legal risks, you will analyse the potential impact in direct financial and indirect (non-financial) terms. Your impact analysis is used to evaluate legal risk as a specialist risk category, and to model and prioritize legal risks against other enterprise risks. We apply some commonly used methods to analyse legal risks that reduce the impact of subjective bias and lead to much richer data. We detail how to use these methods to generate rich legal risk data sets that will lead to a clear call to action at business head and board level. In a world where budget and time are limited, you need to prioritize legal risk mitigation projects alongside other initiatives to ensure that risk management budgets are allocated to projects that will deliver the best return.

Risk management models

Our own legal risk management framework (detailed in this chapter) is an adaptation of two classic operational risk management frameworks from the United States and Europe. If you have an operational risk management framework in place, it is more than likely that it will be based on either COSO's 'Enterprise Risk Management – Integrated Framework' (originated in the United States) or ISO 31000 'Risk management – principles and guidelines' (created by an ISO working group). If you have started to implement legal risk management as a discipline, you may also have seen Australia/New Zealand Standards organizations' 'HB 296:2007 Legal Risk Management', which adapts ISO 31000 to the context of legal risk. Our methodology adapts what we see as the best elements of each of the COSO and ISO models, and combines them with experience of real-world implementation in legal risk.

ISO 31000 'Risk management – principles and guidelines'

ISO 31000 (created in 2009) describes risk management as a process of five sequential tasks supplemented with two continuous activities that wrap around the risk management exercise. The five sequential risk management tasks are:

1. *Establish the context.* The standard can be applied in many contexts, from the charity sector to sports team management, for example. In business, however, the context would be the enterprise as a whole, and include specific risk areas such as operational risk, credit risk, market risk and legal risk.
2. *Identify the risk.* The second task is to establish where risks exist in your defined context. For legal risk, we have already defined our taxonomy in Chapter 1, so for this stage you would identify which of your business practices, products or services could result in financial or reputational loss.
3. *Analyse.* The third task is to estimate the impact of the risks on your ability to achieve your objectives. Specifying the type of impact you care about, and the level, is a key part of this step.
4. *Evaluate.* When you have identified and analysed your risks, you need to compare and contrast the potential impacts, and prioritize risks for treatment according to their relative potential impact.
5. *Treat.* The fifth and final task is to implement controls that will minimize the risk – or eliminate it altogether if that is the appropriate action.

The two activities that you should carry out throughout the process are: 1) Continuous monitoring and review: the principles of circularity that you read about in the last chapter apply here too. You should monitor the risk, make sure it is being managed according to the treatment plan, and review whether the treatment is having the desired effect. If the treatment plan is working, you can revise the original impact rating. 2) Continuous communication and consultation. You should also check for new and emerging risks, meet regularly with stakeholders to re-analyse and re-evaluate your legal risk portfolio, and keep the legal risk register relevant to current activities.

COSO

COSO (established in 2004) takes a slightly different approach to the ISO standard. Rather than focus on a specific risk type it reviews the entire enterprise and identifies eight management components that collectively manage your exposure to different risks. The eight components are ubiquitous in risk management and match much of what we've discussed so far in this book:

1. *Internal environment.* These are your values and policies and how they affect risk decisions, as discussed in the last chapter.
2. *Objective setting.* A very sensible first step is to articulate the objectives that your business wants to achieve, for example 'annual growth of 5 per cent over the next three years,' or 'outpace competitors by 10 per cent'.
3. *Risk identification.* List events that could adversely affect your ability to achieve your objectives; alternatively what events, if you managed them particularly well, would help you to improve on your original goals. COSO makes a distinction between a risk and an opportunity, possibly to give risk managers in the United States (with a more entrepreneurial spirit) the chance to add to the top line, rather than be a constant bottom-line cost-management team.
4. *Risk assessment.* Estimate how likely it is that the event could happen, and what would be the impact if it did.
5. *Risk response.* Decide what you will do in response to the potential risk. Will you 'avoid' the risk entirely, 'accept' it as a possible cost of business, 'share' it by partnering or insuring against specific outcomes, or 'reduce' it through management and control activity.
6. *Control activities.* Outline the policies and procedures you need to implement to ensure that your selected response is carried out.
7. *Information and communication.* Capture and communicate relevant information that affects risk management decisions and activities.
8. *Monitoring.* Continuously evaluate whether the risk management activities you implement are effective, and whether new events and risks could affect your ability to achieve your objectives.

Although it has eight components rather than ISO's five steps, there are clear similarities between the two methods and you will undoubtedly encounter derivations of each in your career as a legal risk manager. Our own method, designed to encourage proactive legal risk management, borrows from both.

Our proactive legal risk management framework

Both the COSO and ISO frameworks have much to offer. The COSO framework gives priority to the overall objectives that your business is trying to achieve – something that can become easily lost in the minutiae of day-to-day operational and legal management. The ISO framework has a more task-oriented approach that matches, to a large degree, steps 3–8 of the COSO framework. Whichever framework you use, it needs to be adapted to account for the specific nuances of legal risk. There are peculiarities to legal risk in its ethical interpretation, moral foundations and behavioural action that require some finesse.

Figure 3.1 Our five-step legal risk management process

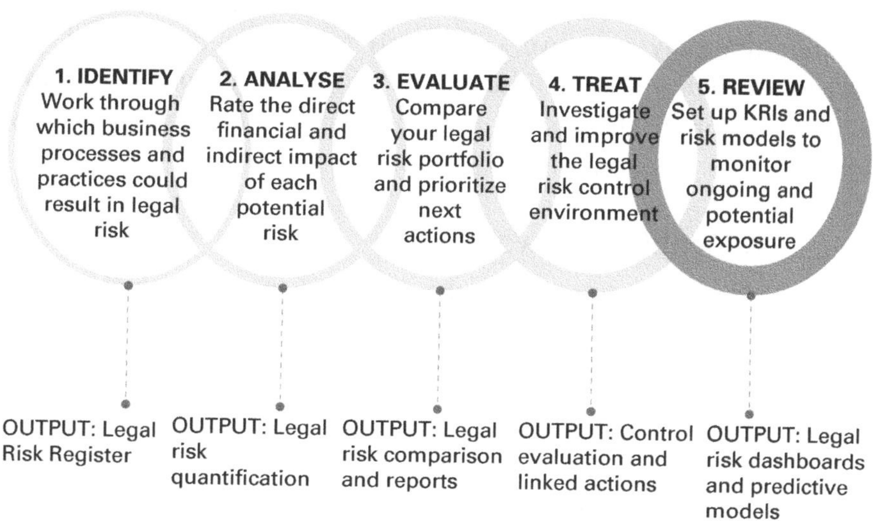

Our legal risk management framework, shown in Figure 3.1, incorporates elements of COSO, but is adapted primarily from ISO 31000 and the ANZ Handbook HB 296:2007. It distils a complex management method into five straightforward steps:

1. *Identify* – identify and map legal risks within each business line and internal function.
2. *Analyse* – estimate the potential impact, financial or otherwise, of the risks identified.
3. *Evaluate* – consider the control environment and enterprise-wide risk and prioritize treatment of the risks based on risk versus reward.
4. *Treat* – implement risk reduction strategies that are proportionate to the potential losses identified.
5. *Review* – monitor how effective your risk mitigation is, and review your risk map against real-time loss data.

Below we work through how to deliver this five-stage process, step by step.

1. How to identify legal risk

The first step, to identify legal risk, is to articulate the ways in which it can be realized in your business. In Chapter 1 you learnt how to create a mutually exclusive, collectively exhaustive set of legal risk categories that will guide discussions within the business, and give sufficient depth to discussions about legal risk to capture potentially all legal risks that you are exposed to.

Legal risk identification workshops

We've used the taxonomy from the end of Chapter 1 as the basis for a legal risk register, shown in Table 3.1. The first column contains our five top-level categories and the second column the second-level categories. You can use this register as a guide to discuss legal risks, and as a tool to capture all relevant legal risks for your business.

Table 3.1 Sample legal risk register

Risk Category 1	Risk Category 2	Risk-specific Narrative
Contractual risk	Unintentional waiver or amendment	*Risk that we could lose our contractual rights through failure to enforce against delivery schedule*
	Unintended consequences from amendment or waiver	
	Failure to use standard terms	
	Inadequate or unclear terms	
	Unenforceable terms	
	Failure to enter into a binding agreement	
	Lack of awareness of contractual terms	
Legislative/regulatory	Failure to adequately comply with legislation/regulation	
	Failure to correctly assess the impact of legislation/regulation	
	Failure to monitor changes to existing or new legislation/regulation	*Failure to carry out regular horizon scanning could result in failure to comply with unknown changes in legislation*
Non-contractual rights	Failure to protect our non-contractual rights	
	Failure to enforce against infringement of our non-contractual rights	
Non-contractual obligations	Unintentional assumption of duty of care	
	Failure in duty of care to clients	
Dispute	Failure to protect privilege in advance of, or within, a dispute	
	Inappropriate resolution regime or strategy	
	Failure to adhere to dispute timelines	

To discuss and identify legal risks for a business line, geography, product or service, gather together a group with expertise in the law, the business under discussion, the internal risk management set-up and an expert facilitator. Much of the knowledge you need is contained in the in-house legal department and we've conducted many exercises where just the in-house legal team have been present. However, when you include a more varied group you often get a more rounded perspective and more accurate identification and quantification of potential risks. Expert input from someone who manages a particular product development process, for example, will add great insight to the potential for legal risks to result from that activity; experts in credit risk can help quantify losses that could result from contractual failures in asset finance.

The role of the facilitator is to keep discussions on track and ensure the group reaches conclusions that can be recorded on your risk register. Without an expert facilitator, risk identification meetings can quickly descend into chaotic, but interesting, discussions on who 'owns' the result of the risks rather than where the risks originate. Your facilitator will be responsible to read down the list of legal risk categories, get the group to discuss their application and add narrative to each potential instance in the business. This is unglamorous work, but provides a vital foundation to the analysis, management and reporting efforts that follow.

In the third column in Table 3.1, you would write specific narrative on how the risk applies within the context of the business or internal function that is the subject of the review. There are good reasons for aligning risk identification to a business line/function. Each business and function will have a 'head of' who is responsible for managing costs and delivering objectives. He or she has the budget and the incentive to take meaningful action when presented with a list of potential losses – and ideas to prevent them.

We've added a couple of example narratives in the risk register in Table 3.1. Try working through a version of your own, and see how each level 2 legal risk category could apply to your part of the business.

2. How to analyse your legal risks

Risk analysis requires you to estimate how likely each risk is to happen and what the consequences would be if it did. One of the most prevalent risk impact analysis methods is the 'impact vs likelihood' matrix, shown in Table 3.2. Although such matrices are widely used, the lack of analytical rigour involved means that although risk ratings can be arrived at very quickly, they are often the result of subjective discussions – 'if that is a 4, mine must be a 3' – that result in poor assessments. We have heard them described as 'better than nothing', but possibly not by much!

Table 3.2 A typical 5×5 risk impact matrix

Impact vs Likelihood	Unlikely	Slightly likely	Likely	Very likely	Certain
Minimal	1	2	3	4	5
Some	2	4	6	8	10
Moderate	3	6	9	12	15
Heavy	4	8	12	16	20
Severe	5	10	15	20	25

An even worse iteration you may find is when the event likelihood scale is replaced with a time-scale, for example to represent a 1 in 2, 1 in 5, 1 in 10 or 1 in 50 year event. This appeals from a quantitative perspective as it maps easily to capital models, but it leads to false confidence in the predictive data that feed those models. We have no way to reliably predict whether a plausible but very unlikely event could happen tomorrow, next year, or in 50 years from now. Based on the principle of 'garbage in, garbage out' – that the quality of the data you get out of a model can be no better than the quality of data you put in – capital models that rely on these types of estimates are flawed. We will talk a little about potentially new ways to model legal risk towards the end of the chapter.

Typical vs extreme scenario analysis

Around 2010 in the UK, there was a movement to add financial analysis to impact ratings, in the hope that this would help organizations to more accurately model their capital requirements. This is a more complex analytical method that requires more thought and takes more time. Because the quantification relies on the judgement of individuals with vested interests in risk numbers reducing, the method wasn't entirely trusted by prudential regulators. As a result, many organizations reverted to the five by five matrix discussed above and this proved to be a missed opportunity to encourage robust, analytical scenario analysis across all risk management disciplines.

However, within the discipline of legal risk, because the potential losses are a product of complex ethical and moral frameworks, as well as being so huge, we find that the only way to get a genuine estimate of potential loss is to analyse two scenarios, typical and extreme, and gather the best possible data set to support the analysis and improve the accuracy of current and future impact estimates. The map in Figure 3.2 outlines the steps you need to take to analyse typical and extreme scenarios for legal risk.

Figure 3.2 Scenario-based impact analysis

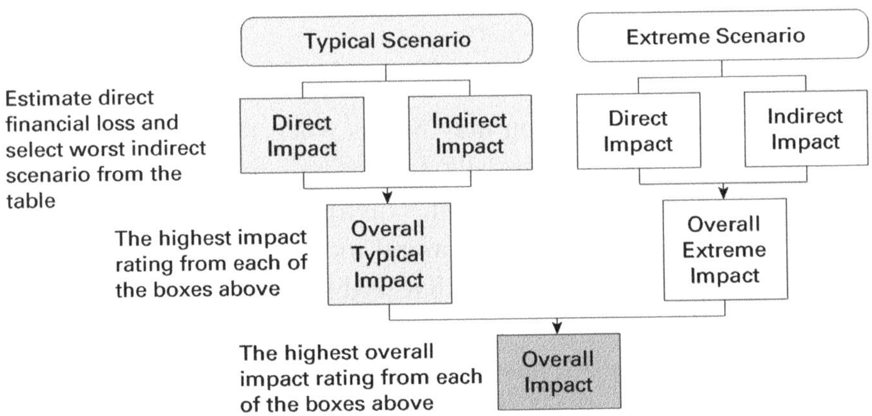

The quickest way to get to a fact-based impact analysis is to use pre-defined scenarios. Scenario-based models give the richest vein of data and analysis and, for our purposes, two simple scenarios will prove to be sufficient:

a *Typical loss.* What is your expected 'typical' loss, taking into account your knowledge of the control environment, over a time horizon of one to two years? This can be cross-checked against operational risk loss/incident data, to give an accurate number. Exposure in this scenario is also known as 'residual' risk in many models.

b *Extreme loss.* What level of loss is associated with the worst plausible, no matter how unlikely 'extreme' set of events, including control failures and external events? This is similar to 'inherent' risk in many models. There is no need to try to predict 'when' the event could happen. It is enough to know that it could happen and at any time.

A note on extreme scenario analysis

Extreme scenario values can give an excellent business case to the in-house team to invest in solutions to resolve the root cause of legal risks, reduce overall exposure and free-up resource in the legal team to focus on new issues. However, they are the estimates that people find the most difficult to predict with any degree of accuracy. Here are two examples that may help.

First, it is tempting, when thinking about headline regulatory breaches, to assume that the worst 'possible' event could happen, rather than the worst 'plausible'. For example, potential fines for breaches of anti-bribery and corruption laws are massive. They could be anything from £50 million to £100 million, or even more if breaches are the result of wide-scale systemic corruption. But if your company has invested in enterprise-wide training, and verified that all employees have received and understood the training, set out clear policies and guidance and invested time and money, then it is implausible that they would suffer a fine of that magnitude. The regulator would take into account the investment in protection and restrict fines to much lower payment of proceeds. The individual would take the blame.

Second, breaches of contract should be easier to think about in an extreme scenario. You will have good data about past losses and the potential for commercial challenge. By extrapolating the number of disputes you see in a typical year, and multiplying it by a plausible factor (×10, for example) you can quickly come up with a plausible extreme loss estimate.

How to measure direct and indirect impact

Direct financial loss is a straightforward measure: what do you expect to lose, based on past losses and your understanding of current business practices, over the next 12 months to two years? Most in-house teams are able to estimate this with some degree of confidence, and actual operational loss data can be used to verify initial estimates. All that then remains is to convert your direct loss estimates to a standard impact rating between 1 and 4. To take this last step, compare your loss estimates to financial loss thresholds that you consider to be minor, moderate, significant and severe, for each of the typical and extreme scenarios. A simple set of risk thresholds is shown in Table 3.3.

Table 3.3 Example legal risk thresholds

	Typical	Extreme
1. Minor	10,000	100,000
2. Moderate	30,000	500,000
3. Significant	100,000	2,000,000
4. Severe	400,000	5,000,000

Indirect loss analysis relies on a scenario matrix

After you have rated the direct financial loss, you need to consider the risk of reputational damage or other forms of indirect loss that are impossible to put a hard financial value against with any degree of confidence. To estimate indirect loss you need a matrix of potential scenarios, with four or five gradations of impact. Table 3.4 grades impact on a scale of 1 to 4, equivalent to 'minor', 'moderate', 'significant' and 'major'.

To use the matrix, for each of the categories in the left-hand column, read across the row and select the scenario that most closely matches your own estimate. Your overall indirect rating will be the most severe across all four categories. To help bring the different scenarios to life, imagine how they would map to the internal escalation levels within your company: which of the scenarios could be dealt with by the person who identified the risk, which might need to be

Table 3.4 Indirect impact matrix

	1	2	3	4
Reputational	Local headlines over a short period	National headlines over sustained period	International negative headlines	Sustained international headlines
	Limited number of complaints	Increased customer complaints	Individual customer action, class action possible	Widespread loss of customers and class action likely
Regulatory	Possible interest from regulators	Heightened interest from regulators, potential investigation	Regulator investigation, probable fine and public censure	Regulator fine and potential closure of business or withdrawal of product
Customer service	Possible minor impact on customer service	Short-term loss of service limited to individual product/service line	Short-term loss of service across multiple product/service lines	Sustained impact on customer service
				Significant loss of customers

escalated to a department manager, which to a business manager, and which to the board.

To create a typical, extreme and overall impact analysis, use the tools provided above to create a calculation table something like that shown in Table 3.5. Because the risk impact is always 'rounded up' to reflect the most serious level of impact, your overall legal risk analysis will probably (although this is not always the case) be dominated by your extreme scenario analysis. To take account of this in your reports, split your reporting by typical and extreme exposure. This enables you to see what your day-to-day legal risk environment looks like, through your typical scenarios. And it enables you to use the extreme scenario analysis to identify which legal risk areas should receive additional investment, to augment the control environment and so reduce the plausibility of the extreme scenario and limit the extreme exposure.

Table 3.5 Sample legal risk impact analysis calculation

	Typical	*Comments*	**Extreme**	*Comments*
Direct	**£10,000**	*compare to threshold table (3.3) = 1*	**£500,000**	*compare to threshold table (3.3) = 1*
Indirect	**2**		**3**	
Overall typical and extreme	**2**	*(highest of two typical ratings)*	**3**	*(highest of extreme ratings)*
Overall risk (highest of typical and extreme ratings)		**3**		

3. How to evaluate your legal risks

When you've identified and rated each risk, you will end up with a register similar to Table 3.1, but with impact ratings in another column next to the risk-specific narrative column, and a business- or geography-specific column to the left of the risk column (see Table 3.6). The

Table 3.6 Example legal risk evaluation table

Business Line or Internal Function	Risk Category 1	Risk Category 2	Risk-specific narrative	Typical Direct	Typical Indirect	Extreme Direct	Extreme Indirect	Overall
Purchasing	Contractual Risk	Unintentional Waiver or amendment	Risk that we could lose our contractual rights through failure to enforce against delivery schedule	10,000	2	500,000	3	3

purpose of the legal risk evaluation is to inform enterprise-wide risk priorities by reporting information and trends about your legal risk exposure. This is where you will get the benefit from following a mutually exclusive, collectively exhaustive taxonomy.

The 17 descriptive legal risk categories aggregate up to enable you to report legal risk exposure in a number of different ways, and to a good level of detail. You can evaluate exposure across legal risk categories: for example you should be able to identify the total contractual risk exposure across all business lines or all geographies, and how this compares to dispute risk exposure. Or you can evaluate overall legal risk exposure across different business lines. These types of aggregate data are what get the attention of senior management, and the additional detail that you have across each of the five pillars will give you information to pinpoint specific issues senior management need to deal with to reduce exposure to legal risk. The detail also gives you data to prepare you for the types of question that will follow. What is it about our contracts that expose us to risk? What can we do to reduce our extreme exposure to legislative/regulatory risk? How does this exposure compare to other risk types?

Because you follow a quantitative analysis and put direct financial values against legal risk exposure, you will be able to evaluate overall legal risk exposure against other types of enterprise risk. Enterprise-level evaluation enables you and your board to prioritize action to reduce risk exposure where it is most needed. If legal risk exposure is a small fraction of credit or market risk, for example, it would be crazy not to augment credit or market risk controls as a first priority. It's also possible that you will identify a number of legal risks across a business process that, when evaluated collectively, represent a significant control issue for another form of risk. For example, a lack of awareness of contractual terms, practices of unintentional waiver of contractual rights, and the presence of inadequate or unfair terms in contracts could all add up to outsourcing risk, supply chain risk, or even credit risk (if you rely on contractual protections that are unlikely to be upheld by the courts).

The purpose of the evaluation is to prioritize actions to mitigate areas of legal risk. Risk mitigation relies on your ability to implement effective legal risk controls that are aligned with your corporate values. When you have identified your highest priority legal risks, you will assess the control environment for each risk to highlight areas that need attention, and prioritize legal risk control augmentation within enterprise risk budgets.

4. How to assess and improve your legal risk control environment

Each legal risk that you identify should have a set of controls to mitigate it. Controls typically take the form of value statements, policies and procedures that you read about in the last chapter. If this is your first legal risk assessment, you will probably want to restrict your control analysis to the risks that expose you to the greatest potential loss. If you have identified risks with a high typical loss, deal with those first to eliminate profit leakage. Then – or in parallel – review the policies, procedures and working practices that are in place to manage the biggest extreme risks, and assess how effective they are as a risk management tool. After you have actions in progress to reduce your priority exposure, continue to work through your list of legal risks until you have mapped controls against them all.

Each control you identify must have an allocated owner, and someone with responsibility to monitor whether it is being applied effectively. Assign management and monitoring responsibility to individual roles, rather than individual names, to ensure that controls continue to operate even when key control managers leave your company.

Table 3.7 has columns for 'Control effectiveness' and 'Reason'. You will rate how effective each control is on a scale (effective, needs improvement, ineffective) and give reasons for the rating. Both your rating and your reasons are recorded to show that the risk management process is being carried out in support of senior manager attestations, and to support actions to augment the control environment.

Table 3.7 List of control ratings

Risk reference	Control	Manager	Monitor	Rating	Reason
Unique risk reference	*Brief description of control*	*Role responsible to manage*	*Role responsible to monitor*	*How effective is the control?*	*What is the evidence/reasoning for the control rating?*
Ref 123	Contract review procedure	Head of Contract management	Chief Legal Officer	Effective	Key Risk Indicators (KRIs) all indicate effective process
Ref 124	Health and Safety Policy	Health & Safety Manager	Audit	Partially Effective	Incidents recorded on Site 24 indicate heightened risk range
Ref 125	Legal Policy	Chief Legal Officer	Chief Legal Officer	Ineffective	No notification to legal department of five disputes entered into in last 12 months

Action plans

If a control is rated as either 'ineffective' or 'needs improvement' (this can also be referred to as 'partially effective'), you must detail one or more actions that will improve the control and therefore reduce your residual exposure to the legal risk. Actions must be assigned to individuals and the action plan must include dates by which the action is expected to be complete (see Table 3.8). Your plan is likely to be audited, so ensure that your actions will have the desired effect and are backed up by realistic and robust project delivery plans.

Table 3.8 Example action plan

Risk	Control	Action	Assignee	Status	Delivery Date
Risk ref	*Control ref*	*Details of action*	*Individual responsible*	*Not-assigned, assigned, complete*	*Date action should be complete*
Ref 125	Legal Policy	Include specific requirements to notify legal department when a dispute is possible	CLO	Assigned	[set date]

Control theme analysis

There are specific actions you probably already take to manage legal risks within each of the five legal risk categories. For example, legislative/regulatory horizon scanning procedures are likely to be a core control within legislative regulatory risk. Trademark and copyright management procedures, and brand management, will be core within the non-contractual rights category. Your contract governance framework would be expected to manage multiple contractual risks, ensuring you capture the right positions, execute correctly, and manage rights and obligations throughout the life of the contract. Of course the value statements set at board level and globally applicable policies that encourage moral behaviours are equally important as key legal risk controls.

A way to shortcut the control review is to group risks together under these types of common process, and then review controls that are in place to manage each process. After you've worked out how to improve the central control theme, you can unwrap the process and record the actions against every risk in a particular group.

Supervisory control framework

Supervisory control frameworks map every senior management responsibility within your organization to the risk controls and processes that are in place to deliver them. For the General Counsel, these will be a mixture of legal risk responsibilities and more general management responsibilities such as management of staff and budgets. General Counsel Supervisory Control (GCSC) frameworks enable you to best place responsibilities for legal risk management in the operating structure of your own organization. You can find a brief example of a high-level supervisory control framework in Table 3.9.

Table 3.9 Example General Counsel Supervisory Control Framework (GCSCF)

Direct responsibility	Supervisory responsibility	Delegated responsibility
Department budgets	Ethical conduct	Compliance (delivery)
Staff performance management	IP Management	Debt collections
Legislative/regulatory monitoring and assessment	Compliance (design)	Employment law matters
Transaction advice and delivery	Contractual rights and obligations management	
Dispute management		

Legal risk control reviews, and in particular the decisions you make on which controls you have direct management responsibility for and which are delegated, provide a robust foundation to your supervisory control framework. (We discuss this further in the next chapter, in the section that explains how to structure the legal and compliance departments.) As a general principle, if you are a General Counsel you need to clearly state what you are directly responsible for, what you have supervisory responsibility for and which risks you have fully delegated responsibility for. You may for example fully delegate responsibility of employment law monitoring to the head of HR, or compliance with law and regulation to a head of compliance – although we don't recommend that.

5. How to monitor and review your legal risks

You have two key tools to monitor and review legal risk exposures: your staff and your operational data. There is no substitute for staff, and your lawyers in particular, interviewing people throughout the business, talking about legal risks and evaluating the controls that are in place to manage them. You should set up a schedule of structured interviews that will enable you to monitor ongoing exposure and review risks in response to business events. When you review risks with a business head, discuss the particular legal risks that apply to his or her business, and details of the control environment that is in place to manage those risks. This will focus the interview on the areas of highest risk, and the controls that need to be improved to reduce exposure.

Risk review interviews

You should aim to review your legal risk register roughly every 12 to 18 months. You will need to create a set of structured interview questions (see Table 3.10) and sit down with your heads of business, and people on the shop floor, to review both the exposure and how effective the control environment is. Your questions will align to the last review, and incorporate changes in business over the last period (we would hope that your lawyers are aware of all changes and feed into them at the proposal stage). The interviews are a good way to reflect on the last year and to discuss new ways to partner with the business to help them to manage their legal risk exposure – and avoid legal loss.

Table 3.10 Sample questions for structured interviews

Interview question	What you would hope to find out
How do you satisfy yourself that legal risk appetite acts as a real constraint to action?	How robust the GC or senior manager thinks legal risk framework is, how well it is communicated and what information they use to monitor
How many of your contracts have an auto-renewal clause that will be activated this year?	Whether interviewees have a good view of their contractual estate, and actively manage them
Do your most important suppliers get the best terms?	Whether teams take a three-dimensional approach to contracting and supply chain management (see Chapter 6)
How many contracts does your business enter into in a typical year?	Whether there is a general contract management process in place
How many deals did your sales team negotiate last year? What deviations to standard terms and conditions did they sign up to?	What level of governance is in place for sales negotiations
How do your product development team test their products for the intended market segment?	Whether there is robust governance related to product design and sales strategy
What is the biggest cause of disputes against the business?	Any potential problem areas and whether there is a general awareness of litigation issues

Key Risk Indicators

Key Risk Indicators (KRIs) are data points that give some guidance on whether specific controls are proving effective at reducing legal risks. To pick effective KRIs, identify potential data points generated by your operational processes. You will most probably need to implement some sort of data processing system or manual procedure to generate KRIs, but the effort is worth it in the long term. The ability to get early warnings of potential legal risks will enable early mitigating action that could save your business millions (possibly billions) of pounds. KRIs can be reporting as single indicators, eg 'contract value', but usually give better information when they are paired with related data points. Some examples of KRI pairs are:

- *Contract liability vs contract value* – a running total of liability versus value, when broken down by contract type, third party, etc, will give good indications of how much risk you are taking on to win particular areas of business.
- *Volume of contracts executed vs volume of deals entered into system* – this KRI will tell you whether you are entering into deals without having a binding agreement in place.
- *Product sales by sales person vs compliance training registers* – this KRI will give you an indication of possible exposure to conduct-related risks around duty of care to customers. If your top sales teams haven't completed their compliance training, or regularly complete it late, they may not be aware of the latest issues in legislative regulatory compliance.

Key Performance Indicators

Key Performance Indicators (KPIs) give you an indication of how well teams, or controls, carry out their objectives. For legal risk, it is the performance of the legal and compliance department that is particularly important. These departments will between them have a direct or supervisory responsibility for the majority of legal risks you identify. Those risks that they aren't responsible for should be acknowledged as 'fully delegated' to evidence that they have been thought through and put under the care of the right department.

The next chapter discusses the role of the legal and compliance departments in some depth, and recommends how to structure them to best effect. Legal and compliance departmental KPIs can include a wide variety of measures and some that we have seen include: feedback from business units, budget performance against plan, litigation volume over time, number of compliance 'near misses', number of IP challenges, customer complaint volumes, feedback from regulator supervisory teams, committee membership, and hours of legal skills training delivered. What is important is that you pick KPIs that can be supported with meaningful, current data, and steer away from measures that create a cottage industry to gather the data.

Legal risk modelling

Apart from KRIs, which most organizations continue to struggle with, the biggest hole in current legal risk management is the lack of modelling and predictive analysis employed by businesses and in-house legal teams. Too many in-house legal and risk teams are content to complete their risk assessments, submit their reports and carry on with their day-to-day tasks without changing much in the way business is run – and won. If this is to change, there needs to be widespread adoption of predictive legal risk models that will bring focus to legal risk management efforts and help to relate real-time, practice-based data to the board. Unfortunately, the current risk models available to legal risk managers are at best seriously flawed, and at worst fundamentally broken.

Traditional risk models are based on 'normal' (as in 'normal distribution') statistical modelling that can be used to predict the tallest human being, or the probability that you will reach 100, if you have already reached 75 (much greater than if you are only 40). Normal models can give accurate predictions of some natural phenomenon, such as measuring deviations from a standard height of human beings, average age and weight distribution across a population of mongooses. However, normal statistical models are unreliable in predicting 'unnatural' phenomenon, such as maximum flood levels on the Nile, or operational or legal risks.

One possible solution to the inadequacy of 'normal' models may lie in the field of fractal geometry, a branch of mathematics invented by Benoit Mandelbrot in 1963. It has proven more accurate in predicting complex phenomena that originate from non-normal patterns. It has been demonstrated to be widely found in nature and economics, used to predict maximum flood patterns in the Nile, highs and lows in the financial markets, cardiac rhythms, cancer incidence, commodity price trends, and seismic geological behaviour (Mandelbrot and Hudson, 2006). Fractal theory is used by the Bank of England to model potential market movements and guide policy. It generates more realistic models of stock variation, for example, and is potentially much better able to cope with the fact that the financial markets suffered several 'once in 100 years' events in the last five years. Regulator fines patterns (see Figure 1.2) show similarly fractal foundations and we believe that fractal techniques can be developed and used to not only predict potential extreme legal loss events in the market, but also to layer data about how well a business is managed to predict your business's ability to navigate these newly stormy waters.

Capital models should reward businesses that have good corporate governance and robust legal (and operational) risk management in place. Changes proposed to bank capital models in 2016 (BIS, 2016) attempt to reward banks with low historical losses through reductions in future capital; banks with high losses would be forced to set aside more capital to offset future risk. Although the approach aligns with our own perspective, in its original form it contains a simplistic relationship between past and future losses that will we hope be improved in the final version. We believe it is possible to use multi-fractals to model the effect of good operating practice on your ability to survive external market crises. The method is unproven, and possibly speculative, but the potential for financial services institutions to free up operating capital and for prudential regulators to measure the operational 'riskiness' of systemically important firms is alluring.

This would be a good area for future research and development. As a rough guide to how to approach this, you could first collect and collate loss data that relate to the legal risks in our (or your own) legal risk taxonomy. These loss data will enable you to design two fractals, the first based on your typical loss (that relates directly to current operational practices) and the second based on your extreme loss (that relates to your extreme scenario analysis). You would then apply a multi-fractal model that uses your 'typical loss' fractal to modulate your 'extreme loss' fractal, and so generate a model to predict your potential future legal loss.

Summary

Fractal modelling is a step into the future. To identify and quantify legal risk today you need to adapt standard operational risk methods to this new and unpredictable risk area. There is much to be learnt from the two most commonly used risk frameworks, COSO and ISO 31000; our own legal risk framework takes elements of each and adapts them to the nuances of legal risk. Our method consists of five sequential tasks: identify, analyse, evaluate, treat and review. You first identify the legal risks that your 'business, its relationships, processes, products and services' expose you to. Your legal risk definition and taxonomy are the foundational tools to use. Second, analyse the potential impact of the risks on your business objectives – in our definition the possibility for them to result in 'financial or reputational harm'. Analyse the impact in terms of two scenarios: what you expect to lose and what you could lose in a worst plausible scenario. When you have analysed all identified risks, you can evaluate them as a group – by business, by geography or by legal risk category – and then evaluate them across the enterprise-wide risk portfolio to prioritize control improvements based on exposure.

Proactive treatment of priority risks is the objective of legal risk management. Controls are typically policies and procedures, but teams and in particular the legal and compliance teams must operate effectively to minimize exposure to legal risk. In particular, your GC Supervisory Control Framework is a core tool to allocate responsibility for legal risk management throughout the enterprise. Implement effective KRIs to monitor the legal risk environment and give early warning of potential legal risk incidents. Implement KPIs to track the performance of the legal and compliance departments, both crucial for day-to-day legal risk identification and management. Also, in an ideal world, implement some sort of predictive legal risk modelling, based on your quantitative scenario analysis and loss data, to predict future legal risk patterns and modify your current working practices to minimize their impact on your business.

The practicalities of legal risk identification cut across a wide gamut of legal disciplines and business areas. In the next five chapters you'll read best practice in how to manage the risks within each of our five legal risk pillars: legislative/regulatory risk, non-contractual obligations (duty of care) risk, contractual risk, dispute risk and non-contractual rights (IP) risk. The contents of those chapters will help guide your interview questions, identify priority legal risks, and implement best practice legal risk management and controls throughout your organization.

PART TWO
An in-depth review of legal risk and how to mitigate it

Legislative/ regulatory risk and the role of legal and compliance

04

Introduction

Legislative/regulatory risk is a top priority for firms in financial services (Whalley, 2016). The pressure on businesses to operate transparently within the rule of law, and the remit of regulators, has increased greatly since the financial crisis. Failure to comply with law and regulation carries serious consequences, but compliance is not an exact science. Because the law is intensely moral in its goals, the way it is applied is complex and open to interpretation, particularly across different jurisdictions.

These complexities are one reason legislative and regulatory risk management is a resource-intensive and costly activity. The law is voluminous, as well as complex: the number of laws and regulations printed each year grows at an astonishing pace. As law and regulation fragments globally, multinational corporations must ask already overstretched legal and compliance teams to prioritize compliance with one piece of regulation over another. There are significant risks inherent in this approach and to avoid making the wrong judgement requires a coordinated approach between legal and compliance teams and a concerted effort to implement pragmatic, fact-based prioritization of legislative/regulatory risk and compliance.

In this chapter you will read first about the issues that make legislative and regulatory compliance so problematic, followed by practical tips to manage our three specific areas of legislative regulatory risk: adequate awareness (through horizon scanning), impact assessment, and adequate/proportionate compliance. These activities are often distributed between legal and compliance teams, and when legal and compliance teams work effectively together they act as an effective line of defence against legislative/regulatory risk. If the working relationship between these two teams breaks down you are likely to find gaps in responsibility that lead to unmanaged exposure to legal loss, or you will find excess duplication of responsibilities and excess management costs. Because your legal and compliance departments are your key line of defence against legislative/regulatory risk, discuss how to structure and manage these two core risk control functions to avoid unmanaged exposure to legal loss and maximize the performance of your legal department.

The increasing burden of legal and regulatory compliance

The law is broad in its moral foundations, and is at the same time incredibly detailed in its technical implementation. If your business trades across multiple geographies, you have to navigate not just your own country's legal systems but a number of systems equivalent to the countries you trade with, and within each country there is a trend to write increasing numbers of laws and regulations. In the United States, for example, there are 50 state legislatures and countless more counties, cities and municipalities. Many of their bills conflict with or supplement federal law, and add layers of regulatory complexity. Experts estimate that it would take a particularly dedicated individual 100 years to learn just the US financial regulatory regime (Wood, 2014).

The increase in volume is multiplied for each jurisdiction you operate in or trade with. There are around 320 legal jurisdictions worldwide, based on one of three foundational legal systems: Common law (eg United Kingdom, United States, Australia and India), Napoleonic (eg France, Italy, Brazil and Spain) and Roman-Germanic (eg Germany, Russia, the Netherlands and Sweden). Businesses that trade in multiple jurisdictions need to be aware of the laws in each jurisdiction in which they operate and how the application of individual laws varies across each jurisdiction.

Two more factors add to the complexity: tiering and layering. Domestic legal systems are multi-tiered, to take account of business diversity, and across international boundaries legal systems are layered over each other, as each domestic jurisdiction tries to impose its laws on companies operating into and out of other jurisdictions. The combined effects of application, tiering and layering have resulted in a rapid increase in the volume of law since 1997. Allen and Overy's Global Law Intelligence Unit (Wood, 2014) estimates that the volume of law has increased by a factor of 1,000 over the last 200 years. They predict that this volume and complexity will increase in line with world trade volumes – and possibly double in the next 15 years!

How to stay on top of legislative regulatory horizon scanning

In this vast and complex legal landscape, staying on top of changes in law that might affect your business is a daunting task. There are some excellent legal information services on the market that will help, and law firms are also a good source of knowledge. Westlaw, Lexis Nexis and Practical Law Company are the best known legal information services in the United Kingdom and United States, but they cast a wide net and you need to pinpoint changes that are relevant to your specific business, in the jurisdictions in which you trade.

Your external legal advisers can be a great source of help when you need to focus on industry- or product-specific legislative regulatory changes. Many large law firms employ paralegals and professional support lawyers whose job it is to monitor, assess and report on the potential impact of changes to law and regulation. They monitor pieces of legislation throughout the legislative process, and are often connected to the legislative bodies. They will quite happily – and occasionally for free – provide you with regular updates that will help you meet your horizon scanning responsibilities.

Note: Because the volume of law is so great, it is reasonable for your General Counsel (GC) to outsource horizon scanning for legal areas that have a restricted level of impact to teams within the business. It is reasonable, for example, for the HR director to have primary responsibility for keeping on top of employment law, and he or she could use his or her own network of law firms or information services to do this. One caveat is that the GC should maintain supervisory control over the process, and review the results of the horizon scanning regularly with the HR director to ensure he or she is getting the information needed and that it is being correctly interpreted.

Using law firm publications and know-how teams

Law firms are generally very happy to provide updates on legislation, regulation and case law. If you are lucky enough to have a panel of law firms, you are perfectly within your rights to ask them to provide regular updates on specific areas that will affect your business. The only problem is that if you ask 10 law firms to provide an update, you will get 10 different formats, so you need to be proactive and tell them how you want them to measure and report the impact on your business. Give them standard tools so that you can collate the results centrally. The methods and tools detailed in the next section can be applied effectively be external legal advisers to give your internal legal teams succinct, draft impact assessments for discussion and review.

Regulatory change and lobbying teams

One way to manage the risk of changes to law and regulation is to exert influence throughout the legislative process to moderate the real-world impact of laws that are usually drafted in the abstract. Many businesses engage actively with the legislative process, not to divert law-makers from their efforts to create a just society but to prevent them from inadvertently creating situations that make compliance impossible. One example where this consultation process was particularly effective is the 2011 UK Bribery Act. In its original form, the Act had no concept of proportionality. Businesses of all sizes and in all markets would have had to implement the same level of internal controls at costs that were entirely disproportionate to the real-world risks. The concept of proportionality was introduced by lawyers in the United Kingdom, in consultation with clients, and made it possible for businesses of all sizes and scope to comply with the requirements of the final legislation.

Another example, this time from the United States, is FATCA. FATCA was designed to ensure that US citizens weren't able to avoid paying tax to the US government by holding assets overseas. In its original form, the act required non-US banks to actively contact every single customer, and get them to check a box to say that they weren't a US citizen. It even resulted in Swiss banks disclosing US account holders for the first time. In its original form, the need to contact every customer regardless of nationality, and pay withholding tax for those who didn't check the right box, would have cost UK banks hundreds of millions of pounds. Lobbying resulted in changes to the way that US account holders were identified, and the final Act is more cost-effective to implement, but delivers the same end result.

How to take a consistent approach to legislative/regulatory assessment

You will be treated far more leniently when you suffer an incident if you are able to prove that you have done everything reasonably possible to prevent individuals from acting in opposition to the letter and the spirit of the law. This means an investment in compliance and risk management staff, specialist compliance systems and procedures; competency-based training and robust policy management and governance structures. All of these activities cost time and money, and the likely volume of legislation and regulations in the pipeline means you probably won't be able to implement all required controls in time.

So your assessment of the potential impact is key to pinpoint your priority compliance projects. Whether you use internal resource within the business, external law firms or regulatory change and lobbying teams, or stick with just your own internal legal team, you need to take a consistent approach to legislative/regulatory impact assessment. There are three factors you should consider when you assess the potential impact of new or modified legislation or regulation:

1. The cost of compliance.
2. The consequences of non-compliance.
3. The timescale to full implementation of the law/regulation.

Impact assessments help you make strategic decisions on where to use your limited resources and budget, and in some cases help you decide whether it makes commercial sense to move into a new jurisdiction or line of business.

Use a scenario matrix to estimate the cost of compliance

It is difficult to put a hard financial value on the cost of compliance with new or updated legislation and regulation. Organizational complexities, inexact estimates of effort, and unknown or uncertain costs, all create factual uncertainties. To cut through these uncertainties, create a scenario-based impact table (albeit based on subjective judgement) to measure consistently the effort required across business lines or geographies. The example in Table 4.1 uses three scenario categories:

1 *Impact on resources.* Questions to ask are: Will you be able to absorb efforts into an existing team? Will you need to take on contractors to cope with a peak in demand, or are you going to have to take on teams of permanent staff/outsource permanently?

2 *Skills and competencies.* Do your staff have the right skill set? Will you need to invest in training, compliance learning and systems?

3 *Systems and processes.* Are your existing systems good enough, or will you need to change them or implement a new system? Will you need to embed new processes, or will changes be absorbed through adjustments to existing procedures?

Using this type of scenario-based assessment matrix enables individuals within your organization – or external advisers – to make judgements based on similar criteria. This consistency allows you to compare and contrast legislative impact assessments centrally, with greater confidence.

Table 4.1 Matrix to analyse cost of compliance

	Rating		
	1	2	3
Impact on resources	Work can be accommodated within existing compliance team; no long-term impact	Work will require temporary additional contract resource, to cope with peak in demand	Work will require permanent resource increase, or long-term reliance on outsourcing arrangement
Skills and competencies	Work falls within current expertise of team	Some additional training may be required for existing and/or new resource base	New training required for existing and additional resource base; additional compliance learning systems
Systems and processes	Work can be accommodated within existing systems; some minor changes may be required to existing processes	Existing systems will need to be updated; process changes will be absorbed through adjustments to existing procedures	Investment in new compliance systems or significant upgrade to existing systems; new policies need to be embedded in corporate governance and supported with additional new procedures and processes

Consequences of non-compliance

The second factor to measure is the consequence of non-compliance. To capture this, define a range of potential scenarios and the relative grades of seriousness. We've included a simple three-level gradation to measure regulator priority and time horizon in Table 4.2.

Table 4.2 Consequences of non-compliance

	Rating		
	1	**2**	**3**
Time horizon	Long-term priority (3–5 years), 5–10 year implementation period; unlikely to be investigated except for serious repeat breach	Mid-term priority (2–3 years); 3–5 year implementation period; investigation possible in the short-term, if breach reported	Immediate priority and possibly highly politicized; significant investigation almost certain if breach reported
Potential for sanction	Minimal scope for regulator sanction, limited to private censure	Regulator sanction dependent on impact of breach; potential for public censure and fines	Regulator sanction almost certain; potential for limited withdrawal of licence and/or significant fines

Time horizon

The third factor to consider is the timescale for full implementation of the legislation, and whether enforcement is an immediate regulatory priority. Regulators and courts also have limited resources, so they focus on areas they think have the biggest effect, for example on market stability, customer outcomes, or public safety. Depending on your sector, competition, health and safety, money laundering, environmental issues, bribery and corruption, and tax avoidance are examples where the consequences of non-compliance can be particularly severe.

This is relevant because the timing of your compliance activities can have a big impact on overall costs and is affected by the political priority given by the courts or by regulators to the legal area under question. When FATCA was first proposed, one high street bank in the United Kingdom raced out of the blocks and set up systems to comply with the full Act in its original form. As the Act was diluted, the cost of compliance fell dramatically, so that when a second bank began its activities 18 months later, its cost of compliance was at least 75 per cent lower. In the European Parliament, the process is notoriously slow, with some pieces of legislation drafted over many years. They change as different groups lobby and influence; because this affects the impact you should reassess them every year. In the United States, Congress rushes bills through and they are often voted on without most people knowing what is in them. One US Senator, Rand Paul, proposed a 24-hour cooling off period between the presentation of a bill and voting on it, just to give legislators a chance to read it.

The differences in process and political motivation mean that not all legislation moves at the same pace, or requires immediate compliance. Unless the legal area is highly politicized, you are likely to be given a couple of years at least to get your house in order. Our three gradations of the 'Time horizon' in Table 4.2 cover the priority given to the legislation itself, and whether it is a priority area for enforcement of your regulators.

Note: Don't underestimate the consequences of legislative/regulatory risk on individuals. The current trend for regulators to moralize and to punish senior individuals in big corporations may be couched in the right principle; it may even be necessary to enforce behavioural changes in some of our big corporations – but it must be taken with caution to the rule of law. Moral judgements can often be treated as political expediency, rather than judgements that ought to be grounded in a proper system of justice. The fuzzy boundary around which kind of negligence should be thought of as criminal requires the law and its interpretation to be very mature. We want to avoid the kinds of example where regulators fail to incorporate basic criminal law protections – such as innocent until proven guilty, or the principle of no self-incrimination – into their treatment of individuals who may (or may not) have breached their rules. The various authorities must agree the extent to which people should be liable for the actions they take at work, and decide to what extent criminal sanctions that will ruin individuals' future ability to do their job and to support their family are appropriate. They also must decide whether it is appropriate for regulators in any industry to combine the triple powers of executive authority (write the law), legislative realm (pass the law) and independent judiciary (decide whether behaviours fall within the law).

Legislative regulatory impact reports

When you are asked to report on the key pieces of legislation/regulation that are going to affect the business in the next few years, it is helpful to have a visual model. Tabular timelines can be effective, but the volume of legislation makes them long and unwieldy, and lengthy time-horizons make the information quite static. An alternative is to create some sort of bubble-chart, or radar chart, using the data from your assessment matrix. Your bubble chart could have two axes: cost of compliance on the vertical and consequences of non-compliance on the horizontal. Each piece of legislation would be plotted on these axes and represented by a bubble, and the size of the bubble would indicate how close the legislation is to its final form.

Another way of representing the legislative horizon is the radar diagram. In this instance you would have concentric circles representing the time-horizon (one to three years, three to five years, five years and more, for example). These circles would be divided into segments that are appropriate to your business: four business lines, for example, or five regional areas. Each piece of legislation would be represented by a bubble, colour-coded to represent the combined risk level from your assessment, for example the multiple of cost vs consequence.

How to get maximum value from your legal and compliance functions

The roles of legal and compliance and how they work together are evolving as the legal risk landscape changes. Both departments have key roles in managing legislative regulatory risk, and getting the right balance between them is crucial for effective legal risk management. Because the roles are evolving, it is useful to discuss some of the topics that you would expect a typical compliance department to cover. It is also useful to review the options that are available to you with regards structuring these two key functions.

An outline of the responsibilities of a typical compliance department

Horizon scanning, risk assessment and prioritization tasks are the first steps you take to manage legislative/regulatory risk. They are invaluable if you plan to take a strategic and proactive approach, but the key to protecting your business from legislative/regulatory risk is in the implementation of an adequate compliance programme. Adequate and proportionate compliance with law and regulation is one facet of legal risk where mismanagement can have particularly extreme consequences. Volkswagen's troubles can be put down to a straightforward failure to comply with emissions regulation, for example. Petrobras' problems are an example of a seemingly systemic failure to comply with anti-corruption rules. These are also due in part to cultural failings in each organization, and legal and compliance teams, through their checks, balances, training, advice and reports are an important lever in instilling the right culture in your organization.

Table 4.3 Typical compliance topics

Anti-money laundering and counter-terrorist financing and sanctions	Client money and client assets
Anti-bribery and corruption	Client on-boarding
Conflict management	Cross-border marketing
Data protection	Market conduct
New product/service checks	Regulatory reporting and notifications
Systems and controls	Competency training
Tax	Health and safety
Environment	Human rights

Compliance teams cover a broad range of topics (see Table 4.3) and the breadth and depth of these topics mean that chief compliance officers often need large teams. These teams can represent a significant cost, but that cost is an investment to protect you against the avoidable systemic issues and preventable rogue elements that result in significant legal loss. Compliance teams, as part of their responsibility, will advise front-line employees whether new products are suitable for your planned market, or which regulatory disclosures need to be made in the event of a breach. They also provide compliance training, for example in how to avoid activities that could be construed as bribery or corruption, monitor specific behaviours and report incidents and near misses, and monitor registers to ensure your business teams comply with all relevant rules.

Compliance training

No one really likes to spend their time in compliance training, or legal training for that matter. But if your staff aren't aware of the laws and regulations that affect their role, they could make mistakes that might expose them (and you) to accusations of mismanagement. The quality of the content of your training, and how effectively it is delivered, will be an important aspect of your defence if you need to prove that individuals have acted unlawfully of their own accord, rather than through any form of corporate encouragement.

To be effective, compliance training courses must outline the laws and regulation, the impact on individuals' roles at work, and the consequences to those individuals of non-compliance. You should review regularly the quality and content of your training, and who has taken and passed it. Readily available learning management systems can record employees' test scores and issue reminders to those who have failed to take specific courses that are relevant or mandatory to their role.

Systems and checks

Your control environment, for example using Know Your Client (KYC) checks, help prevent staff from making the type of systemic mistake that can result in senior managers losing their jobs. If your KYC checks aren't thorough, your business could unwittingly and repeatedly breach anti-money laundering legislation. To prevent systemic issues and remove any temptation for staff to act unlawfully, implement robust controls that can only be circumvented by deliberate act, so that anyone who acts unlawfully is doing so deliberately and in clear contravention of corporate policy and practice.

Reporting near misses and KRIs/KPIs

Monitoring Key Performance Indicators (KPIs) and Key Risk Indicators (KRIs) will help you to track how well you are performing on a spectrum, rather than on a binary fail/no fail basis. Senior management need to know about near misses as well as actual loss incidents. It matters a great deal if you regularly come close to processing fraudulent payments or to life-threatening accidents. Reporting near misses helps to focus the mind of senior management and staff on what could happen, and invest in additional controls to make sure that it never does.

How to structure your legal and compliance departments

You have a clear decision to make when you review the structure of your legal and compliance departments. You can either create a structure where there is separate management and reporting for each of them (Figure 4.1 – A) or you can create a structure that has a combined management team and single reporting line to the board (Figure 4.1 – B). It may seem that there is no 'right' answer (and there are pros and cons for each set-up) but we strongly believe that to take a robust and consistent approach to legal risk you need to have a single person responsible. That person should be either the General Counsel or chief legal officer, and should have a direct reporting line to the board executive and report additionally to an independent director on corporate governance and legal risk.

Figure 4.1 Unified management structure (A) and separate management structure (B)

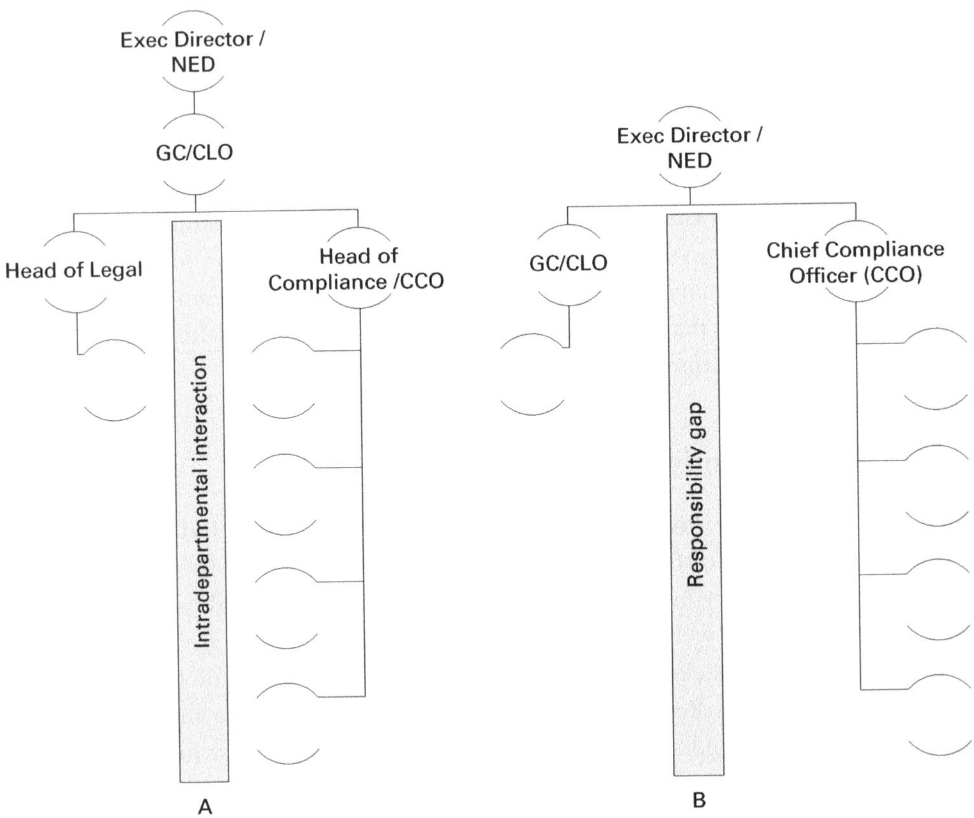

It used to be quite common for compliance departments to report to the General Counsel, but the increased profile of regulator fines, and emphasis on legal compliance, has pushed compliance to the front-of-mind for many businesses. It is tempting in this environment to build up the compliance department, separate it out from legal, and take comfort in having two sets of overlapping reports. New governance models often more closely match that in Figure 4.1 (B), with separate reporting lines for the chief compliance officer straight to the board or a board sub-committee.

There may be some degree of comfort in seeing two sets of reports, or two different sets of personnel conducting an important investigation that could materially affect the company's value. However, duplication of management teams at the top leads to duplication of effort and confusion of responsibilities throughout the two departments. This will at some point lead to issues falling between the cracks and not being dealt with at all, creating potential gaps in coverage of legal risk. If the legal and compliance departments have different senior managers, those managers will have different views on who is best able to handle a matter. Good managers will naturally compete for additional, higher profile and 'more interesting' matters to claim as part of their portfolio. A unified structure and single point of contact at board level will limit the negative effects of politics to an intra-departmental (and entirely normal) level, crystallize key issues and prevent the heads of either legal or compliance passing issues between them.

Apart from the management benefits, there are many projects on which legal and compliance teams best serve your company by working together. Lawyers and compliance officers bring different skill sets to the table. Lawyers are trained in the law and how to interpret it, so can take responsibility for horizon scanning and impact assessments – possibly with help from a network of external law firms. Compliance officers have in-depth understanding of business processes and policy, and the myriad ways in which staff might try to circumvent policy. Regulators may prefer (or even demand) to deal with non-lawyers and so push to have non-lawyers from compliance (or elsewhere) representing the company when attending regulatory meetings. A combined management team gives you the strength to send either lawyers or compliance officers, depending on your own perception of need.

The three core objectives of the modern legal department

The increase in focus on the compliance department has led some legal departments to rethink their own role within the organization. As General Counsel, you want to have a seat at the top table; this is essential if you are to play a full role in managing legal risk in its many forms. Your seat there will be secure if you can clearly articulate how your legal function meets three core objectives:

1. *They must exert necessary influence and control over business decision making.* They influence control over business activities that could result in legal issues for your business, and so must maintain a strong governance role within your organization.
2. *They must deliver effective insight to the business.* To help them become more effective at making long-term, sustainable profits, and navigate the complex global legal and ethical landscape.
3. *They must run themselves efficiently.* Make best use of their own resources and budgets to deliver these insights, and reinforce their governance role within the business.

Below we cover each of the three core objectives in more detail, and discuss some of the key facets within each broad area of responsibility.

1. Governance and control

The mandate and value of the legal function has been debated since the mid-1990s and it seems that many GCs are no closer to resolution. Lawyers are trained as advisers, to sit apart from their clients and not get too involved in the day-to-day running of their business. In private practice this works well, but when lawyers make the move in-house, they must learn quickly how to engage with the business, and to treat the corporation as the client, not the individual. Most important, they must have a mandate to proactively influence business decision making to keep activities within the letter and spirit of the law.

The role of legal in the three lines of defence

The role of compliance in the three lines of defence is widely understood, but the role of legal is widely debated; this may be part of the reason the two departments are so often separated. Regulators in the United Kingdom have been clear since 2012 that they consider the legal department to be a second-line risk management function. In their eyes, legal departments have a clear responsibility to identify and manage legal risk across the organization as a whole.

Because most people usually have experience of lawyers only in their advisory capacity, they are usually employed to advise businesses on transactions or deals, or advise more broadly in niche areas of law as a way to save on outside counsel costs. These specific advisory roles are first-line management roles, and although they are valued by the business they play little or no part in the second line of defence (see Table 4.4). Lawyers are an important part of the second line of defence because they understand the underlying legal issues, and can identify potential areas of individual or systemic legal risk. They will help you to understand which behaviours and decisions are most likely to cost the company long-term sustainable profit, and they can help individuals avoid career-limiting mistakes.

Table 4.4 The varied roles of legal within the three lines of defence

First line	Most companies employ lawyers specifically to advise on business transactions, commercial contract negotiations, etc. This specific task is considered line '1b', or management of front line activities
Second line	In-house legal teams have a responsibility to identify, aggregate and advise the business on how to proactively manage legal risk. This area has been neglected and is where most legal functions are now trying to improve their delivery
Third line	In a very few instances, lawyers will assume third-line internal audit responsibilities. They will check that other legal teams are managing legal risk appropriately, and when they act on internal investigations (fraud or regulatory) they adopt a pseudo third-line audit role

Legal and compliance departments need a firm mandate and clear authority

Even in some of the biggest companies, legal and compliance teams have struggled to secure the necessary authority to act on their own knowledge of corporate misdeeds. This has contributed to the checklist compliance cultures that are utterly ineffective in preventing serious legislative/regulatory breaches. General Counsels, chief legal officers and chief compliance officers must all be given a clear mandate and the authority to do their job. In some jurisdictions and sectors this is a statutory requirement, and any senior managers of a legal or compliance function who feel unable to perform their role must disclose this to their regulators. Align your legal and compliance teams to your business, but operate them under a separate budget and reporting line from business decision-taking teams. They must have clear authority to prevent deals from happening if they have evidence of a material issue that the business is ignoring.

Legal teams must clearly communicate their mandate

Your legal and compliance departments must communicate clearly the need to manage legal risk within acceptable levels. Make the consequences of policy breaches clear, and ensure all employees in your organization are aware of their responsibility to work transparently and efficiently with your legal and compliance staff to protect your company's – and its shareholders' – assets and profits. Very few companies have any appetite for unlawful behaviour, but the complexity of the legal environment and the myriad technical regulations mean that some level of legal risk has to be acceptable.

As a GC, you articulate your mandate through your legal and compliance policies, your legal-risk appetite statements, your set of supervisory responsibilities, participation in performance reviews in the business, reporting lines and operating model and of course through your day-to-day interactions with the business. You should communicate your legal policy and legal risk appetite statement to the whole organization, and make sure that your task-specific legal policies – Amendment and Waiver to Contracts, for example – are communicated and acted on by the front-line teams.

2. Give effective insight to the business

As well as putting the right controls and checks in place to prevent the business from inadvertently exposing you to legal risk, your legal and compliance teams play a role in helping your business to make long-term sustainable profits. They give insight into the legal risk the business carries, opportunities to win work, how to operate effectively, and how to make the best possible commercial decisions in legally uncertain jurisdictions. They should advise on changes to regulatory environments that may help you to maximize your income, and ensure that your negotiation teams get the best possible deals, follow market practice, or innovate new practices to gain competitive advantage.

Reporting to the board

Senior managers, when they report to the board, tend to get bogged down in very detailed discussions about individual material issues. These issues are important, but not as important to the company strategy as trends in overall legal risk exposure and the possible reasons for those trends. If overall legal risk exposure is up by $2 billion for example, because you have been exposed to a significant bribery issue, you can talk specifically about the details of that case and how your team is helping local management to minimize the impact and invest in controls to prevent a repeat incident.

Equally important are the potential future changes that could impact specific parts of the business. Any advice a General Counsel can give the board that will help them to avoid significant legal risks – risks that competitors may miss – could give real competitive advantage to your company.

Business surveys

You should make it standard practice to survey, at least annually, the line managers about their view of the legal and compliance functions. If you don't have a good understanding of the business's view of your department you will have a limited and distorted view of the quality of insight being given, and whether it is useful to the business. This seems obvious, but many major companies and non-profits never ask their managers to seek out comments from the internal clients they serve.

Self-service insight

It isn't always time-efficient to discuss issues in person with the legal or compliance teams. There are many business areas where speed to market, or to close the deal, make a real difference. Legal and compliance teams can help by setting up self-service information or precedent sites that give the business teams the tools they need to close deals quickly, with good legal documents, and in full compliance with law and regulation.

3. Operational performance

The pressure on legal department costs is constant, and entirely justified. Lawyers are notoriously poor at creating and sticking to budgets, but there is no reason why legal and compliance functions should be treated differently to other business functions. They have an equal responsibility to operate within a fixed budget and manage resources to deliver the right level of service to the business at the best practical cost. There may be some truth that it is impossible to anticipate 'all' legal costs, but with good analysis and planning it is still possible to estimate costs with some degree of certainty, and set aside a contingency for unknown events.

Annual operating budgets

Annual operating budgets must be created in detail. Include demand estimates and the resource you need to meet that demand. Some years will require investment, in new technology, teams and external advisers to help realize cost-efficiencies and set up lower cost-managed service centres. Other years you may be able to cut back, possibly due to the positive effects of your legal risk management programme! Whatever your budget is for the year, monitor it and report regularly on performance against that plan.

Internal resource

Your attitude towards resource should reflect that of the business. Waste should be eliminated and staffing should be lean. Deploy the right personnel to avoid duplication of effort, and maximize the speed and efficiency of the process to get to a reasonable conclusion as quickly as outside factors permit. Review whether the premium cost of external advisers results in premium service and expertise. It is possible to save money in the short term by increasing internal resource at the expense of external firms, but if you follow this strategy you will find you need to constantly remind your chief finance officer of the savings you are making relative to your pervious cost baseline. Also, you will need to re-evaluate your strategy if lower cost options become available externally. (For an example of new resource options, skip ahead to Figure 6.3 and read the end of Chapter 6.)

External counsel budgets

The real benefit of experienced in-house counsel should be that they can monitor and question outside counsel about their deployment of resources on legal matters and on litigation strategy. The reality is that in-house counsel too often defer to their external colleagues on legal strategy and budgets. Always ask questions up-front about the expected budget and how it will be spent: there really are no excuses for external counsel not to give a budget estimate at the outset. All projects have the potential to overrun, but the surest way of fulfilling that potential is not to specify a budget at all!

Actively manage 'panel' budgets and 'value-add'

You should consider setting up a 'panel' of law firms, who agree to work at discounted rates, and to provide budget estimates before beginning a matter. As work progresses, your panel firms should give you information about progress against budget, and you can use this as a key metric to evaluate law firm performance. If you use law firms partly for their legal insurance backed up by Professional Indemnity cover you need to work out up-front what the financial value of that protection is worth and manage your budget in line with your bottom line.

If you have a panel of law firms you should also expect to receive 'value-add' business and legal knowledge services and tools as part of those arrangements. Law firm knowledge teams are a great resource but are not always used by clients to their full potential. Contact your panel firms and ask what they can do to help reduce your legal risks.

How to manage the core assets of your legal and compliance departments

In support of these three responsibilities, the modern legal department has three core assets that affect its ability to meet those responsibilities over time:

1. *People and talent.* Your lawyers (and non-legal staff) are the core of your legal department. The skills and knowledge they bring to the business are essential to deliver insight effectively and to exert necessary influence over business decision making.
2. *Technology.* This is possibly the key differentiator to improve legal department operational performance. As a traditionally poor adopter of technology, legal departments can benefit from significant operational improvements for a relatively modest investment.
3. *Structure.* Your structure or operating model needs to support efficient allocation of responsibilities throughout the organization, and lead to clearly defined roles within each of the legal and compliance departments.

The way you manage, develop and deploy each of these assets has a fundamental effect on your ability to deliver within (and beyond) the individual capabilities of your team.

1. People and talent

At the core of your department are your people. At its simplest, your people strategy should be to hire the right people, train them well and make sound strategic judgements about the allocation of resources to deliver insight, improve governance and deliver more efficiently. To do this, you must treat your staff as a resource that can be developed, with investment.

Strategy

Your people strategy should align to the strategy of the business and incorporate fundamentals such as performance management and objectives.

Take on people with management experience, and don't be afraid to hire non-lawyers to support your legal team, as well as in compliance roles. It is surprising how few legal advisory teams contain non-lawyers, and yet how excellent non-lawyers are at delivering clear, concise and insightful advice. Management accountants, for example, have learnt to deliver dashboard reports to inform management. Project managers have developed methodologies to deliver huge global projects on time and within budget. These talents – and many other non-legal skills – can be a great benefit to a team of lawyers.

Investigative skills and compliance knowledge

An often overlooked set of skills is how to obtain information from both humans and documents. Interviewing witnesses in a way that is firm but friendly to tease out the full story is a surprisingly rare skill that is not easily taught. Regular staff training sessions using relevant fact and legal scenarios can improve, or keep sharp, this vital set of skills for legal and compliance staff alike.

Sharing investigative knowledge and skills between legal and compliance departments is one way to resolve potential conflicts. Some compliance officers will have the requisite legal background and/or business training to make better investigators, depending on the nature of the investigation. For example, they might understand exactly how your business dealings are structured, and so more quickly investigate actions that may or may not constitute bribery or sanctions violations. Skill sets will also vary depending on whether the issues are likely to turn purely on 'the facts' (favouring a compliance role) or on the interpretation of law and regulation (favouring a legal role). The insistence of some regulators that they prefer to engage with non-lawyers means that compliance personnel (or line managers) will need to be heavily involved in (but not necessarily 'in charge' of) regulatory investigations. Instil a culture of skill sharing across teams to get the right balance of skills on each individual investigation.

Relationship management and 'soft skills'

It is fair to say that legal and compliance staff aren't always the most approachable of teams. The legal profession isn't the most user-friendly, and compliance staff are often trained to say 'no' rather than to think through issues and work with the business to find a route to 'yes'. Developing your staff's influencing and presentation skills will help them to convince the business that they are a strategic and valuable asset, and get them involved in business discussions at a much earlier stage.

Legal expertise and business knowledge

Obviously it will be very useful to have one or more lawyers with substantive expertise in the various legal issues the company regularly faces: eg bribery, sanctions and money laundering statutes across the various countries in which the company operates. Equally important is the need to hire or retain staff who are familiar with the details of how the business operates, or to invest in staff rotation to embed deep business knowledge in your department. That knowledge is essential to uncover innocent – or intended – deviations from proper behaviour among the staff; especially if your business is particularly specialized or technical.

On the compliance side, encourage skilled, experienced and well-respected individuals to transfer from the business. They will help existing staff develop their knowledge, and improve the profile of the compliance department with that business line.

Risk management

Very few in-house lawyers, or lawyers generally, receive formal risk management training. This is likely to change as legal risk management becomes more prevalent in legal education, and specialist legal risk courses become available to current executives. At the very least, you should set up cross-functional teams to review what skills are required and how to deliver them, and encourage your lawyers and compliance officers to attend your firm's operational risk training courses.

2. Use of technology

The legal sector isn't known as an early adopter of technology. There are still anecdotes in private practice about partners who use their computers as paperweights! However, from 2014 onwards there has been an increase in new versions of technology solutions aimed at the legal market. These include matter management systems, e-billing and even artificial intelligence and robotics. Wherever you are on the technological adoption spectrum, when you make smart investments in good solutions that serve an identified business need, you will create a more efficient and much happier place to work.

Matter management

One of the core tasks of the legal department is to process 'legal matters'. These are small or large packages of work that require input – and often management – from the legal team. A matter could be a piece of minor advice on some contractual language in a new template, or a multi-billion dollar global lawsuit. Collecting data on each matter, and in particular the potential legal risk exposure, will add to the management information used to guide senior management decisions. Data collection is unglamorous, but vital if you want to employ any of the legal risk models that we covered in Chapter 3. It will also help you, or your legal management team, to make data-driven decisions about staffing levels and resourcing options. There is great power in being able to prove that your team is operating at 100 per cent capacity – and that they have been doing so for the last six months. If you take report data straight from your matter management system, you can remove the time-consuming need for your lawyers to give regular, detailed reports on every twist and turn in resolving a matter.

Matter management systems used to be large, cumbersome beasts that had to be installed on your own corporate IT infrastructure, and could take up to 12 months (and often longer) to install, configure and get working. Nowadays, mobile-friendly systems are available in the cloud that take a few weeks to get working – from the date you e-sign the contract!

Management information and reporting

One of the best uses of senior lawyer time is to set and communicate the strategic direction of the legal function, deploy resources for optimal performance, and anticipate new legal risks in the business. You need data to support these strategic decisions and to inform the insights you give to the business. If you follow our advice to create KRIs to feed legal management dashboards, and KPIs to monitor the performance of your own team, you will also need to deploy technology to automate the monitoring and analysis, or at least to generate interesting reports that speak to the underlying issues. KPIs could include analysis of budgets against plan, law firm spend against performance rating, and benchmarking data that you can use to compare your own performance against that of similar functions. KRIs you would hope to extract from business data systems, possibly using some sort of robotic process automation tool, or artificial intelligence engine. Technology will help you avoid asking your legal team to duplicate effort to gather and collate data manually that is already being gathered by other teams.

Contract robotics

Contract robotics is a new area of legal technology that began to emerge in 2014. It involves the application of Artificial Intelligence (AI) to analyse, extract and process unstructured data within contracts. It sounds space-age, but in 2015 UK law firm Berwin Leighton Paisner created and won an award for building the first contract robot in the United Kingdom (Limited, 2016). The robot processes basic real-estate documents, but does so 10 million times faster than a human being. The time and cost savings add up to triple-digit returns, and the use-case only scratches the surface of what the technology can do. AI technology is evolving rapidly, so if you have any teams that review and amend the same types of contracts every day, explore contract robotics vendors to see how they can help you.

3. Structure

Your department structure needs to support cost-effective delivery of insight to the business, and support a clear articulation of the scope and responsibility for the governance and oversight you have over business decision making.

Resourcing model

The most basic (and probably most obvious) need when managing costs is to minimize staff deployed on any given matter or type of matters. There are few matters where internal resources beyond one senior and one junior staff member are necessary to handle the investigation and/or defence. If larger resources are truly needed, then outside counsel (or other consultants) should be retained to handle the matter. Unless you have a low-cost internal resourcing strategy, the number of internal resources should remain low on any given matter unless it is, for example, a global investigation of some company-wide practice or behaviour.

When it comes to work that crosses between legal and compliance responsibilities, deploy staff based on the skill set needed for the particular matter. Your structure should lead naturally to that result, assuming you have one person ultimately responsible for making those decisions.

Legal operating model

At the heart of the legal function is the legal operating model. Your model sets out the work that you are responsible for day to day, the work that you have partially delegated to another function but are responsible for monitoring, and the work for which you have delegated full authority to another team. This type of model is also known as a 'supervisory control framework'.

Your operating model articulates allocation of responsibility within the legal department, and interactions with other departments. Your model must support your ability to influence core business decisions, and to manage key legal risk areas to prevent the company from suffering any form of legal risk-related loss. Figure 4.2 sets out a basic template that you can adapt. To flesh this out, label the business units and internal functions that you support, then list the risks that you manage for each business line and function and the specific responsibilities you have to manage those risks.

Figure 4.2 Simplified Target Operating Model (TOM)

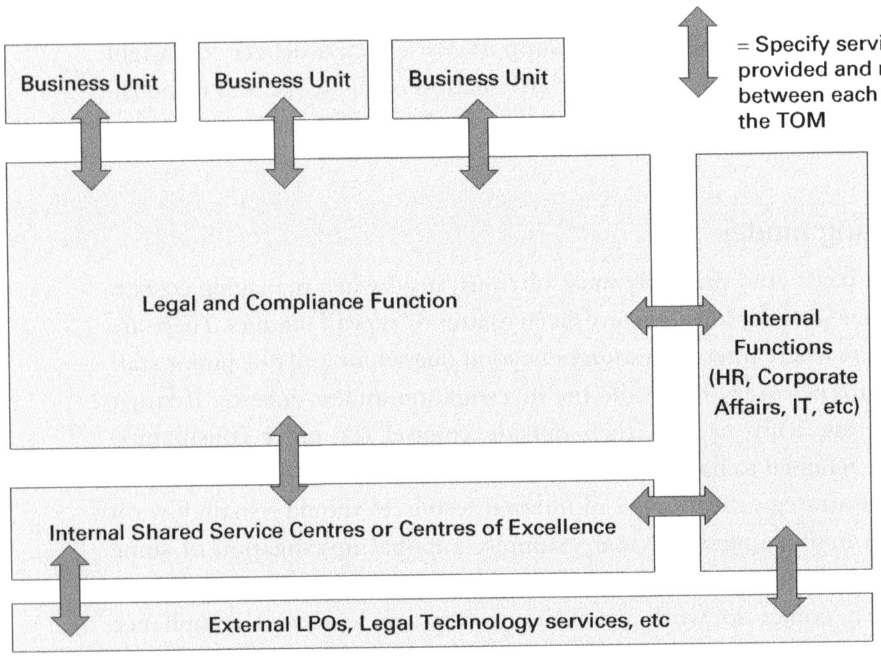

Roles and responsibilities

To define your function's role and individual areas of responsibility in a framework is a relatively straightforward analytical exercise, and is a critical obligation of senior management; implementing that framework can be far more complex and controversial. The potential for conflict and politicking with other departments is high. The interaction between legal and compliance is obviously important to the management of legal risk, but you also need to articulate your working relationship with other functions, business lines and geographical management teams. This will ensure that legal risks are covered throughout your organization, and responsibility and authority for action delegated appropriately.

Use of non-core resources

To deliver efficiently, you will need to plan which resources will be non-core, or non-aligned to a specific business. 'Shared-services' teams and 'Centres of excellence' deliver similar services to multiple internal teams, and can provide a consistency to cost ratio that is difficult to match with a core team. Add to these your planned use of dedicated legal process outsourcers (LPOs), approved panel law firms and legal technology providers.

Summary

The legal and regulatory environment is complex and voluminous. If you operate across international borders you must navigate multiple tiers of interacting legislation and regulation, in volumes that are increasing each year faster than an individual person's ability to read them. There are myriad opportunities for your staff to fail to comply with the law, intentionally or otherwise, from board level to the shop floor. Compliance failures are likely to result in sanction for your organization, and possibly criminal sanction for the individuals involved. To cope with this volume and complexity, you need to take a practical and pragmatic approach to legislative risk assessment and prioritize legal and compliance resource to the most significant identified risks, as well as to investigate and minimize the impact of breaches.

Apart from the external factors of volume and complexity, probably the biggest risk you have to manage is the working relationship between your legal and compliance teams, and their combined relationship with your business. Employing trained and experienced lawyers is expensive and you will want to get value from your investment in those departments. To do that you need to ensure that an effective management structure is in place that encourages the best use of resources between the two departments, and minimizes the chances that legal risks will fall in between gaps in responsibility. We are advocates of a combined function, led by a General Counsel who reports to the board executive and separately to an independent director on matters of governance and legal risk. There are other options you can explore however.

We've discussed typical topics covered by compliance, and our own perspective on the objectives of the 'modern' legal department. The focus on governance and control, business insight and operational excellence set clear expectations and give a structure within which senior management can begin to deliver consistent performance. Most important, your legal department should have a clear mandate to manage legal risk, and be integrated fully into your enterprise-wide governance structure. There should be no contradiction between your business strategy and goals, and your company's conformance with legal and ethical obligations. Legal and compliance departments are an essential lever in your ability to achieve this balance. In an environment of increasingly complex legislative and regulatory requirements, they are an essential element of your company's ongoing commercial success.

Non-contractual obligations 05

Ethics, conduct and duty of care

Fiddling with risk appetite pales in comparison to the task of turning away human beings from bad behaviour.

Introduction

One aspect of legislative/regulatory compliance that is particularly difficult to accomplish is the need to operate within the 'spirit' as well as the 'letter' of the law. Most extreme legal loss events are the result of a breach of non-contractual obligation – or failures in duty of care to third parties. The legal risks come from an area of law known as 'tort', which is as close as we can get to a definition of the 'spirit' of the law. The primary aim of tort is to discourage individuals from doing things that could hurt others, and so act as an efficient form of risk deterrence against non-criminal, but harmful, acts. At their most simple, non-contractual obligations put a responsibility on you (as an individual as well as a business) to think through the potential outcomes of your actions and put in place protections to prevent adverse harm to third parties. The risk is that you may be found negligent, and failures in duty of care are a focus of legal courts and the enforcement divisions of regulators.

In financial services, regulators' approach to enforcement against companies found to be negligent in their duty of care has changed significantly since 2012. The level of sanction imposed on firms show the dangers to a sector, or an individual business, when a gap is allowed to develop between prevalent business practices and contemporary regulatory attitudes. Firms in financial services failed to grasp the shift in ethical perspective and the way their actions would be judged not just by the regulators but by the press and the public alike. The reaction to this has been to focus on corporate culture (as you read in Chapter 2) and in particular 'conduct risk' as a way to positively influence behaviour within firms. Regulator enforcement isn't peculiar to the financial services sector of course, and you will read later examples of how regulators from other sectors have focused on duty of care since the 1990s. To stay proactive in this area, you need to know more than just what regulators say they are going to do: you need to try to stay ahead – or at least not too far behind – their thinking. To do this, you need to embed principles of ethical interpretation into the decisions you take every day.

When the European Banking Authority put ethical conduct within the scope of legal risk in 2015, it brought into focus the role that in-house lawyers can play to positively influence business decisions throughout your business. Because lawyers are trained in professional ethics, as well as how to interpret the law, they have a keen sense of when behaviour is 'right' or 'wrong' and, because ethics don't deal in absolutes, they can give guidance on the degree of 'right' and 'wrong' in different decisions and how they might be interpreted in the future by regulators or the courts.

The one area where professional ethics is put at the focus of not just the professionals that work in it, but the entire sector, is healthcare. Ethics in the healthcare professions has evolved in light of scrutiny from a number of stakeholders, so looking at it in some depth provides insights into the complexity of professional ethics and a template against which ethics in legal risk can begin to be interpreted. Throughout this chapter we will draw on developments in ethical interpretation in healthcare to show how to proactively manage this area of legal risk.

To begin, we will focus on the root of this risk type. We will define duty of care, detail a template based on the US courts that will help you to define where you might have particular risks if you fail in your non-contractual obligations, and give some guidance on how to prove or disprove causation between your actions and the harm suffered by a third party. It is often difficult to predict whether a duty of care exists, it is sometimes difficult to prove that a third party has suffered harm, and it is always difficult to prove (or disprove) conclusively that your actions have in some way caused that harm.

There are four areas of focus for duty of care

It isn't always obvious whether you have a duty of care towards a third party. Even legal courts find this difficult and in the United States have struggled quite openly even with allocating direct duties of care. When the California Supreme Court concedes in frustration that it cannot predict duties, it is unsettling *(Dillon v Legg, 441 P.2d 912,916 (Cal. 1968) quoting William L Prosser, Law of Torts 353, 3rd ed. 1964)*. Each day, the courts enforce sizeable – sometimes bankrupting – judgements against 'duty-violating' defendants without a clear and logical foundation to their reasoning. For those readers outside the United States, we should point out that when it comes to the law of tort, the approach of US courts is considered by lawyers to be a mess, and we've included a few cases at the end of this chapter that highlight the confusion. The US courts drive many of the more significant sanctions, and their regulators are also some of the most punitive in the world, so they are a good jurisdiction in which to study the extreme impact of non-contractual obligations risks.

The first step to assess impact is to establish which third parties you could have a duty of care towards. We classify four broad areas:

1. *Environment* – for example the effect of your actions on natural habitats, or the local populace.
2. *Market* – for example your duty to protect a competitive market; fiduciary duties.
3. *Stakeholders* – for example your duty to create a safe working environment for staff, or to protect shareholders' interests.
4. *Customers* – for example your duty to provide products that are as described and fit for purpose.

Each area has a specific set of laws and regulations that set out a structure for acceptable behaviour, for example environmental law or consumer law. So you could argue that these risks are legislative or regulatory in nature. However, in these areas specific laws and regulations are designed to prioritize specific types of adverse outcome, and they are therefore not comprehensive. The courts aren't able to predict where new types of risk could materialize, and so deal reactively to prevent future recurrence of past events. If you focus on compliance with existing law and regulation, you run the very real risk that your current actions will be viewed as negligent at some point in the future.

Seven factors to help you decide whether you have a duty of care

Sometimes duty of care is easy to establish. Intentional facilitation of a crime is an obvious breach, for example, that will result in criminal prosecution. Manufacturers are strictly liable for defective product designs, even if another person is the direct cause of an injury from using the product. General Motors discovered this when it failed to disclose a known defect with its ignition switches, which meant people could disable the front airbags while the engine was running and increase the likelihood of death and serious injury in the event of certain types of accident. This resulted in compensation being paid for 124 deaths, recall of nearly 30 million cars, and payment of $900 million as part of a Deferred Prosecution Agreement with the US Department of Justice. General Motors' legal department was aware of the issue and failed to act with urgency to ensure the disclosure was made. This is one of the most serious failures in legal risk management that we've heard of, and we hope that other legal departments will learn from the lessons of that case.

Not all cases are so clear-cut, and as a legal risk manager you need to try to stay ahead of what the courts might decide. You need to predict in advance where your standard business practices, as well as the decisions you take, subject you to specific duties of care that could expose you to financial or reputation damage if you were found to be negligent in that duty. Predicting potentially illogical behaviour may sound impossible, and it won't be helped by the occasional tendency (in the United States particularly) for plaintiffs' attorneys to create novel causes of action in the pursuit of windfall profits. However, the California Supreme Court (CSC) has detailed the seven factors it considers when making judgements about tortious claims. We will use the CSC as a template but bear in mind that courts in other jurisdictions apply different tests. The CSC template may be useful as a predictive or preventive guide, but it is not a definitive guide to how judges in other international jurisdictions will treat a claim when it is heard in their court.

Under California's test of duty, a judge should consider seven tests when they are establishing the basis for a case under tort. Read through each test, together with the comments of how each test could inform your own possible risk analysis.

1. The extent to which the transaction was intended to affect the plaintiff

This gauges the extent to which you intended harm to the third party. In the workplace, this could be particularly applicable in employment cases – bullying and harassment, for example.

2. The foreseeability of harm to the plaintiff

Could you be reasonably expected to be able to predict in advance that an adverse outcome could result from your actions? Forward-looking risk assessments are a way that businesses try to predict adverse outcomes to third parties as well as to themselves. If you carry out extreme scenario analysis in line with our methodology in Chapter 3, and the adverse outcome isn't identified, you may well have built a good defence.

3. The degree of certainty that the plaintiff suffered injury

It is not always certain that the person bringing the case suffered actual harm to the degree claimed. This concept will resurface in Chapter 7 as understanding the 'quantum' that is under dispute.

Proving causality and certainty of injury are the traditional requirements for recovery. You need an objective process for framing the appropriate scope of the cause A and effect B at issue in a particular claim. You then can assess by evidence-based methods whether a risk exists as a general causal proposition. It will then be up to the trier of fact to assess through the introduction of case-specific evidence whether the plaintiff's individual circumstances meet the general pattern of that risk. This assessment process is one of the weaknesses of the courts in the United States, but remarkable advances in informatics and database searchability provide greater access to data-based evidence to support objective judgements about causal 'knowledge' without relying on popular, unfounded or incompletely founded opinion.

Later in this chapter you will read about regulator prioritization of tort. In these cases, your regulator is likely to have studies that prove adverse outcomes result from specific behaviours – the UK's Financial Conduct Authority (FCA), for example, has carried out research into the harm caused to individuals who find themselves in excess debt (FSA, 2012). So if you find yourself in a dispute with a regulator in one of these areas, arguing that no harm was or would be suffered will probably be a waste of time.

4. The closeness of the connection between the defendant's conduct and the injury suffered

This is a vague description of the concept of 'proximate cause'. Your ability to prove or disprove the connection between your business practices and adverse outcome will be central to the quantum at stake. Your operational risk management processes and controls could be crucial to your ability to prove that your firm isn't directly or knowingly negligent.

5. The moral blame attached to the defendant's conduct

The judgement of 'moral blame' is rife with uncertainty. It is a factor of the prevalent ethical considerations, which we cover later in this chapter, and the degree to which you have tried to prevent the adverse outcome through effective risk management practices.

6. The policy of preventing future harm

The risk deterrence goal of tortious claims requires judgement about which cases could have the biggest potential significance. Courts will tend to view cases more harshly where they think it is likely that copycat behaviour could follow. Regulators write their own rules about preventing future harm, and they have taken significant strides in changing corporate behaviours in areas they prioritize.

7. Effective judicial administration, including guarding against limitless liability

This principle is considered in order to prevent a flood of litigation and ease the burden on the courts of showing a direct link between corporate negligence and damage to the public at large. This requires evidence to support the degree to which the risk of injury was enhanced by the presence of negligent or intentional harm. If you identify a risk that could result in an adverse outcome to a third party, and take no steps to mitigate that risk, you could find yourself on the wrong side of a significant sanction from either the courts or your regulators.

The seven tests are applied regardless of which of the four broad areas the claim concerns. One line of defence you have as a business is the set of reasonable protections you have put in place to avoid adverse outcomes for third parties.

Regulators prioritize duty of care risks in their enforcement decisions

Regulators create a set of rules (regulations) that interpret the rule of law for a specific sector or specialist legal area. They act as a 'front' to the rule of law and give useful interpretation to individuals on what is acceptable and unacceptable behaviour. They have become particularly effective at prioritizing potential areas of risk and aligning their enforcement mechanisms to those priorities. For example, the US Environmental Protection Agency (EPA) set out in the 1990s to 'target its environmental protection efforts on the basis of opportunities for greatest risk reduction'. This wasn't an empty or temporary statement. In 2015 the EPA imposed sanctions against Hyundai-Kia that included a fine of $100 million, forfeiture of emissions credits and more than $50 million invested in compliance measures. The prioritization from regulators is mirrored in business's operational risk frameworks. Based on our own experience, we estimate that around 75 per cent of the operational risks you manage originate from a duty of care.

In financial services, the US Securities Exchange Commission (SEC), in common with the FCA and Australian Securities and Investments Commission, have all put public trust and consumer confidence at the heart of their work. In June 2015 the European Banking Authority (EBA) included accidental and deliberate or negligent conduct breaches in the scope of legal risk. Because the link between conduct of business and legal risk has been made, you need to articulate the potential causal link between what your company does and potential negative impacts on customers, markets, environment or stakeholders and take proportionate steps to change behaviours that could lead to adverse impacts. The enforcement actions of the FSA, FCA, PRA (Prudential Regulation Authority) and SEC (shown in Figure 5.1 later in this chapter) display quite clearly the step change in enforcement and prioritization of operational and conduct failures. Since 2013, the level of sanction imposed has been raised to a level that incentivizes behavioural change.

The role for lawyers is not just to interpret risk frameworks against the letter of the law or regulation, but against the spirit of the law, and how your current actions could be interpreted ethically in the future.

Risk management data can prove – or disprove – direct causation

> The law does not require precision in foreseeing the exact hazard or consequence which happens. It is sufficient if what occurs is one of the kind of consequences which might reasonably be foreseen.
> *(quoting Brown v. Nebraska Pub. Power Dist., 306 N.W.2d 167, 171 (Neb. 1981))*

There are some areas where your duty of care is very clear, largely because legislation has been drafted specifically to clarify what the expectations are on you to prevent potential harm. Health and safety legislation, bullying and harassment, environmental protection rules, and rules related to rogue trading and misreporting accounts are all good examples of where the law has clarified the rules on specific duties. However, even in these areas it can be notoriously difficult to prove definitively whether your specific actions resulted in the adverse outcome, and whether you will be found liable as a corporation.

For example, if a 'rogue' boss abuses his or her staff but does so in clear knowledge that it is against firm policy and will be subject to disciplinary action if discovered, it is highly likely that the individual will be held personally liable, and your firm will suffer little direct sanction. However, if you have no anti-bullying policies in place and there is a general culture of bullying and harassment in your workplace, you are likely to be found liable as a company, be subject to a significant pay-out to the individual who suffered the harm, and be required to resolve the issues in your workplace. In this example, as a legal risk manager you can quantify the financial and reputational impact of potential employee claims, and balance that against the cost to implement robust anti-bullying and harassment training and policies.

The expanding scope of contemporary risks, the accelerating pace of risk assessment and discovery, and the lack of rigorous judicial tests of liability means that there are many potential risks that are less clear and less easy to quantify. One of your best forms of defence against the charge that you should have foreseen a potential adverse outcome is to provide evidence that you have taken all reasonable steps to review where you could fail to meet your non-contractual obligations, identify sources of potential adverse outcome in each of the four areas of duty, and evidence of the preventive actions you have taken to avoid the adverse outcome. A significant portion of operational risk management practices are designed, in principle, to ensure that your business meets its duty of care, but the lack of understanding of the legal origin of these risks, and the lack of input of lawyers into their management, has left a gap that regulators have focused on through their enforcement actions.

Operational risk management and legal risk controls act as one line of defence against corporate liability. To find a direct causation between an action and an adverse effect requires knowledge of the causal relationship. Evidentiary data isn't always readily available, so in the courts this area of tort has evolved under the auspice of 'reasonable foreseeability' – a woolly concept that is difficult to prove or disprove. Statements of risk contain a causal, numerical and nominative connotation; for instance: there is a 10 per cent (numerical) risk of developing lung cancer (nominative) from cigarette smoking (causal). A risk is based only on causes proven in fact – in other words, that are objectively known on the basis of the best factual scientific or economic evidence at a given moment in time. If you have no causal data available to prove or disprove a direct link between your actions and negative effects on third parties, you are forced to rely in your best reasonable assessment. When you make legal risk assessments in this area, and match your control environment to reduce the potential risk, you are proving that you have taken reasonable steps to 'foresee' the potential for an event that could cause adverse harm – and that you have taken proportionate steps to reduce the potential likelihood of the event occurring and the level of impact if it did.

Regulators may look in detail at your approach to risk mitigation

This intersection between the law and risk management is a fascinating area and one in which lawyers' understanding of professional ethics and the obligation to uphold the rule of law and the proper administration of justice gives them a unique perspective. They can apply this perspective to business decisions where there may be particular tension between businesses' need to deliver profit and the need to balance the best interests of third parties. They can give especially valuable judgements on how the decision may be interpreted in future, and in particular whether that interpretation could result in future regulator sanction.

Many regulatory agencies advise certain actions be taken as a precautionary measure: a 'better safe than sorry' approach. Although in the past, non-contractual obligations risk outcomes were based on poorly or partially informed decisions from regulators and the courts, advances in technology and in particular data analytics mean that decisions today can be made on a better informed, evidence-based approach. Investigations can now audit data trails to discover whether you had any foreknowledge of potential adverse outcomes, and review your risk management and compliance procedures. In the United States, for example, the SEC appointed a Chief Compliance Counsel in 2015 specifically to review a firm's compliance frameworks in the event of a regulatory investigation – to make judgement on whether it had implemented sufficient risk controls.

The ethical lens we use to judge moral behaviour has changed

> Duty – Behaviours either self-imposed or imposed by others with the aim of decreasing harm and promoting wellbeing (better life). (Purtilo, 2005)

The shift in the way large corporations are judged has been driven in part by new understanding of human behaviour that questions the ability of people to make good decisions, and the level of responsibility that corporations should assume for the decisions their customers make. One result of this shift, as you have read, has been for regulators to modernize their enforcement priorities related to duty of care. In their efforts to impose cultural change, they have made the individuals in charge of corporations more personally accountable for their actions and personally liable for any adverse outcome that may result. In the shadow of the financial crisis and many corruption scandals, it is vitally important for corporations (and the executives that lead them) to establish a framework (and a reputation) for voluntary compliance with the spirit of the law, as well as its myriad technical details.

This concept of compliance with the 'spirit' of the law is where ethics and legal risk combine. We mentioned earlier in this chapter that the approach to ethics in the healthcare profession has evolved under scrutiny from a number of stakeholders, and we will take some time here to explain that approach and how it is relevant to legal risk.

Healthcare professionals regularly keep in mind a framework (see Table 5.1) to help them think through how their reasons for recommending particular treatments, and approach to patient care, would be judged when viewed retrospectively. In the emotive environment of a patient consultation, the framework enables them to view their actions dispassionately and to consider implications beyond whether they themselves feel a course of action is the right thing to do.

Table 5.1 Four-factor ethical framework

Autonomy	The principle that individuals have the right, in certain situations, to be self-governing (unless they lack capacity, for example through dementia, drug use or age)
Justice	The principle that equals should be treated equally
Beneficence	The principle that individuals or companies should promote good
Non-maleficence	The principle that at the very least individuals and businesses should do no harm

A framework for ethical interpretation of action

The terms 'ethical' and 'moral' have become interchangeable in general use, but academics make a clear distinction between the two words. Ethics is the study of values and morals. Values can be personal, group/collective (in this book you've already read how value statements apply in the corporate context), or societal (reflected through laws). Values are enacted through moral (or immoral) behaviour. Moral judgements, such as those made by courts or regulatory enforcement divisions, are made against societal norms. The framework outlined in Table 5.1 provides a logical structure to interpret and potentially predict those norms. The discussion in the following paragraphs will help you to form an opinion as to their effect on how your business practices might be judged.

> That ethical interpretation sits above you all the time. (Graeme Copnell)

The four principles aren't binary. The relative weight given to each can shift along a sliding scale, under the influence of a wide range of societal pressures. It is this change that you are trying to predict, because if you can predict the way that regulators or courts are likely to judge your actions, you can improve decision making and working practices within your business to avoid being found negligent in your duty of care.

The balance between autonomy and beneficence is currently in flux

Justice and non-maleficence are core values in society. We have a constant intolerance for actions that intentionally harm others and we believe – and enshrine in law, for example through the Human Rights Act and Equality Act – that all people are equal in their rights. It is usually obvious if your behaviour is contrary to either of those ethical principles, and it is almost certain that if it is you will be found liable in the event that a third party suffered some sort of adverse outcome. If these two principles are broadly constant, it follows that it is in the balance between beneficence and autonomy that you will find the known unknowns. Autonomy and beneficence will always be in tension. It is impossible to actively 'promote good' if you always allow others to make their own decisions autonomously; and the greater the moral responsibility you have for the actions of third parties, the greater is your responsibility to ensure you won't lead them to take actions that may not be in their own best interests.

Because society relies on the law as the ultimate moral structure to review and check our actions, the legal profession clearly has a role to play in proactively assessing whether business practices are within the spirit as well as the letter of the law. In-house lawyers in particular should give their businesses insight to the ethical framework outlined above, and take it into account to influence business decisions and practices towards an acceptable ethical standard.

Behavioural economics has impacted the field of ethics

If you wait until you are told by regulators that what you are doing is wrong, there is a good chance you will have baked immoral practices into your business. The actions your business takes today may be judged more harshly when reviewed in the future, and since around 2012 we've seen a steady shift in emphasis of the ethical concept of autonomy that is very important to note. At this point we should add a caveat: ethical interpretation is influenced by national idiosyncrasies, and if you are reading this in a jurisdiction that has developed a different ethical perspective, you should review your behaviour based on the relative weight of the same four principles in the jurisdiction in which you operate.

In the West, recent advances in behavioural economics are beginning to influence the field of ethics and move health policy towards a more paternalistic (beneficent) viewpoint in areas of health promotion and public health. Since the 1940s/50s, there had been a steady move towards autonomy and in particular informed patient consent. Between 2003 and 2008, because of developments in behavioural science that were picked up and applied by economists to improve healthcare decisions in the United States and the United Kingdom, the ethical pendulum began to swing the other way. The effects of behavioural economics aren't limited to healthcare, however, and although behavioural scientists aren't ethicists, and certainly didn't set out to influence regulators' thinking in any way, their work has impacted public policy and in particular financial regulation. Intentionally or not, they have challenged understanding of human behaviour to a degree that has caused public bodies to question their approach and find new ways to influence the public and enforce standards in financial regulation.

Behavioural economics is a branch of behavioural science that argues that because people are irrational, the economic markets are similarly irrational. It is the result of developing understanding of the way people make decisions, and in particular of the fallibility of human decision making. For many years the commonly held perspective was that people behave rationally and make rational decisions that are in their best interests and based on all the facts available. The Nobel Prize-winning work of Daniel Kahneman and Amos Tversky, popularized in the 2011 book *Thinking, Fast and Slow* proved, through a series of experiments, that the human brain is poor at analysing facts and making rational decisions. In particular, they identified that human beings have a natural and effortless habit of seeing patterns in the world around them, regardless of whether those patterns actually exist, and that they are bad at making fact-based, rational decisions that are in their own best interests. They even proved, through scientific experiment, that the cognitive act of making a fact-based decision can deplete a person's blood sugar levels and result in genuine physical fatigue. The effect can be immediately mitigated by consuming sugary food or drinks, and a colleague and friend once delighted in this fact as the perfect excuse to eat cake at 11 and 3 o'clock!

The full impact of this work on the field of ethics is still emerging, but is potentially quite profound. Their evidence that we base decisions on the nearest available information, and that the way information is presented has a significant effect on how much weight we give it when we make those decisions, has an ethical impact when the consequence of the decisions can be potentially harmful. Banks, for example, are more likely to be held responsible for the financial difficulties their customers experience if there is evidence that those customers aren't able to make good rational decisions about their financial health and circumstances.

The two ethical theories that guide decision making

This is relevant to legal risk. The lines between moral and immoral behaviour are blurred and it can be difficult for individuals or groups to judge their own actions in the heat of the moment. One typical way to judge how your actions might be interpreted is the 'billboard' test: to consider how comfortable you would be to have your decision posted on a billboard outside your office. This sense-check will help guide decision making to a more socially acceptable norm, but it is binary. You can add finesse to these binary judgements by applying two ethical theories that accommodate the four principles you read about earlier.

You can apply either of the two ethical theories of action described below. One of these should be prevalent, depending on current societal norms as reflected in the balance between beneficence and autonomy discussed earlier:

- *Deontology.* Was the action taken for the right reasons, regardless of the outcome? If this theory is prevalent, the outcome will be inferior to whether the act itself is morally sound.
- *Consequentialism.* What was the outcome of the action, regardless of the reason? If this theory is prevalent, the morality of the action is inferior to whether the outcome is positive or negative: the action can be morally justified if the outcome is seen to be positive.

In the world of banking, for example, you could argue that the act of making money available is morally sound, regardless of the individual outcome for the people you lend it to. From a deontological point of view, because the act of lending money is morally sound, you will need to worry less about the consequences for the people who borrow – and so your risk of being found responsible for adverse outcomes for customers is reduced. However, if the same action is viewed from a consequentialist perspective – if someone who borrowed money from you entered a cycle of debt, developed larger problems and lost his or her home – your action in lending them money would be viewed as immoral, because of the adverse effect on the individual. You would be thought to have a greater responsibility for your customer's overall financial wellbeing, and your risk of being found liable is greatly increased.

Although both arguments are logically correct, the argument that wins is the one that most accurately reflects contemporary societal norms. Our observation is that whether or not your business provides services that society needs – oil, gas, finance, motor vehicles, telecoms, technology, etc – the 'moral value' of overall benefit to society is overshadowed by the net effect that delivery of those services has on consumers, markets, staff and the environment. Regulators and public policy makers give preference to outcomes and your overall risk of being found liable for those outcomes may never have been greater.

Nudge – libertarian paternalism in the health sector

In the health service there is great debate about the morality of taking paternalistic (framed in beneficence) actions to improve the choices that people make. For example, two American economists, Richard Thaler and Cass Sunstein, published a book, *Nudge* (2008), that took the insights developed by Khaneman and Tversky and applied them to public policy. They proposed that because people aren't the best judges of what will serve their interests, institutions and governments can help frame information in ways that will 'nudge' them towards better decisions for themselves (and others). The book is an elaboration of a paper they published in 2003 in which they introduced the term 'libertarian paternalism', couched in beneficence. In it they argue that what sounds coercive is actually just a way to make people more effective at getting what they want. This flew – and still flies – in the face of the libertarian (autonomous) culture in the West and is still being keenly debated years later.

These sorts of societal shifts don't happen overnight, and they have multiple causes over and above those discussed here. But this most recent shift does seem to be a result of the twin factors of widespread public distrust of established institutions (the very public scandals involving banks, oil and gas companies, utilities firms, the press, and politicians that have filled the newspapers since 2008 and caused the public to question the morality of what those businesses do), and understanding of behavioural economics within regulators and public policy makers. What you have read about ethical frameworks and behavioural science is not abstract theory. These two areas of social science are applied today in public policy, and frame regulators' thinking across many sectors. We will finish this chapter with a case study that covers one phenomenon that is a direct result of these twin factors: the emergence of 'conduct risk' as a new risk area in UK financial services.

CASE STUDY Conduct risk in financial services

The whirlwind of ethical debate about duty of care, consequence and causality crystallized with particularly striking effect in financial services in the United Kingdom after the financial crisis in 2008. The crisis put behavioural issues in the spotlight – in banks and regulators – and the regulator of the time, the FSA, was split in two five years later. The two new regulatory bodies are the Prudential Regulatory Authority (PRA), which is responsible for stability of the market, and the Financial Conduct Authority (FCA), which is responsible for conduct in the industry. The FCA has gone some way to articulating its expectations around conduct-related issues and non-contractual obligations. It split its focus between three areas:

1. The way information is presented to customers, either in sales materials or presentations.
2. The culture and practices within the firm and in particular whether they support actions that are in the customers' best interest.
3. Firms' efforts to protect customer data and to support a fair and competitive market.

The introduction of increased obligations to customers, as well as data protection and anti-competitive behaviour, has contributed to a fourfold increase in operational risk capital in the eight years following the crisis. The increase has been driven to a large degree by legal loss in the form of regulator fines (see Figure 5.1) litigation expenses (see charts in Chapter 1), reputational issues (see Chapter 1), attritional loss from commercial disputes (see Chapter 7) and the cost and disruption associated with regulator investigations.

The 2011 work of Kahneman and Tversky has informed thinking in the FCA. Its enforcement division has researched the consequences to customers who are encouraged, for example, to get into more debt than they are able to cope with. It put emphasis on banks, insurers and asset managers to test that the products they sell will deliver the described benefit and are appropriate for the person who is buying them. This imposes a greater duty than existed pre-crisis, and one that is enforced through severe, behaviour-changing sanctions, as shown in Figure 5.1. The fines represented by each line in Figure 5.1 have been imposed by one of the FCA, PRA, their predecessor the FSA, and the SEC in the United States. They are imposed almost without exception for operational or conduct failures and in particular for failing to put in place adequate procedures and policies to prevent negative outcomes for either consumers or the market in general. The issues are wide-ranging and include rogue trading, benchmark rate fixing, IT failures, client money handling, bribery and corruption failures and mis-selling financial products.

The FCA is particularly interested in ensuring that firms take appropriate steps to balance information asymmetry in the markets. It is certain that you will always know more about the product you are selling than your customer. The FCA doesn't expect banks to make available every piece of information they have (this would only confuse customers and lead potentially to further enforcement action) but it does expect banks to share relevant information simply, in a way that helps consumers to make a decision that is in their best interests.

Figure 5.1 The step-change in approach from regulators in financial services

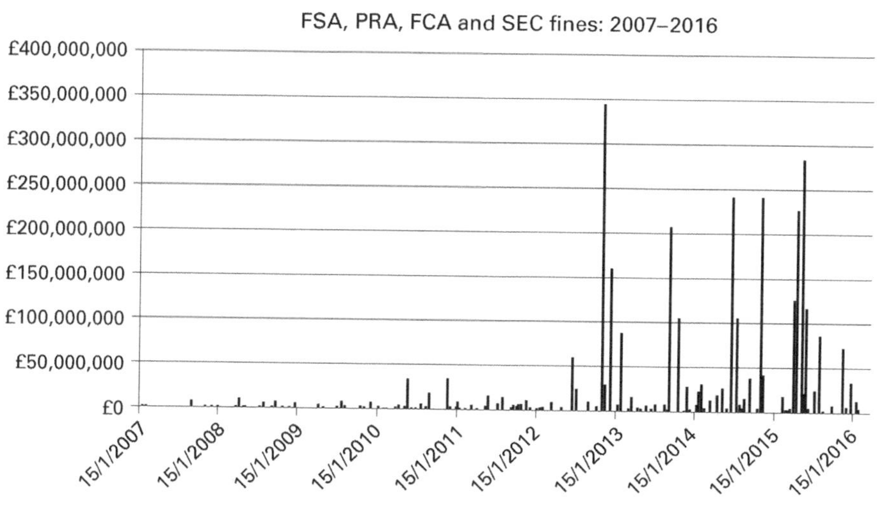

Summary

Non-contractual obligations are probably the most difficult legal risk area in which to assess and predict potential loss. Deciding where you have a legal or moral obligation to a third party can be unsettlingly difficult, as evidenced by the words from the CSC above. To prove whether or not an adverse outcome is suffered as a result of your action – or inaction – is even more difficult to identify and the ethical interpretation of action by the courts (inconsistent and difficult to predict, in the United States in particular) offers little help. There is some guidance you can use to assess where duty of care may exist, and you can read the seven tests that the CSC applies.

The two areas of social science that we've discussed in this chapter, ethics and behavioural economics, are of real and direct use in identifying and managing non-contractual obligations risk in your organization. If you work in a heavily regulated sector, you will be all too aware of the prioritization by regulators of non-contractual obligations risks – although they probably refer to them by another name. If you can stay ahead of, or at least not too far behind, current regulator thinking you can make positive business decisions that are in line with contemporary moral behaviour. You should make particular use of the skills of your legal teams, with their foundation in professional ethics, and learn lessons from the health sector to help guide and influence business decisions.

From a business perspective, the reflection of societal norms through regulatory enforcement is probably the biggest source of extreme loss that results from legal risk. The majority of eye-watering fines imposed by regulators in financial services are a result of firms' failures in their duty of care. The issues that Petrobras, Volkswagen, General Motors and BP have all suffered are also examples of how failures in duty of care can impact your business. Whatever industry you're in, the scale of loss and impact on operations when you suffer a breach sucks up huge amounts of capital and operational resource, and if you can minimize your exposure to this area of legal risk, you can gain real competitive advantage.

Case list

> We are of the belief that every legal problem – whether it concern the 'great issues' of civil disobedience or the humdrum matters of Offer and Acceptance and Last Clear Chance – has its roots and perhaps its analogy in traditionally 'philosophical' realms. Strip away the technical legal terms, plumb the debate's assumptions, and a host of implicit philosophical positions will be found. (Bishin and Stone, 1972)

In this chapter we have stated quite clearly our view that it is unwise to let the courts or regulators decide whether your actions are inside or outside the 'spirit' of the law. If you'd like to read more detail on some 'woollier' verdicts, review the cases listed below.

> Balancing branding efficacy vs social disruption, ie competing ethical concerns. Compare *Crew v. Cloncs, 303 F.Supp. 1370 (S.D.Ind. 1969)* with *Richards v. Thurston, 404 F. Supp. 449 (D. Mass. 1969)*

These two cases are in contrast with each other – each case involved a male high school student suspended during the Vietnam War for having long hair and refusing to cut it short. In Crew, the judge found that the potential disruption to other students meant that the school ban on long hair was justified. In Richards, the court expressly rejected Crew, stating that 'it is absurd to punish a person because his neighbors have no self-control and cannot refrain from violence'.

Taken together, the two cases show that different ethical principles inform judges' attitudes to social symbols like hair length. The same sorts of competing considerations could also come into play when dealing with things like racy brands or advertisements.

> Bookkeeping/financial projections not in line with conventional standards (even if done for personally compelling reasons). See *SEC v. World Radio Mission, Inc., 544 F.2d 535, 537, 543 (1st Cir. 1976)*

A Christian church corporation contended that a religious entity may report aspirational revenues as current assets. Accused of fraudulent accounting, the corporation explained that its prospectus's intended audience was religious. Thus, the corporation reasoned, the audience had or should have had a different understanding than a secular audience about what financially will become true – and thus is presently true – as a result of prayer. The court did not accept this rationale, proclaiming that the prospectus was merely aspirational, not true, and the revenues had not yet come to pass at the time the prospectus was distributed.

> Subtle fraud may be easier for regulators to detect or decree than company insiders. *David Brown, The Press-Release Conviction of a Biotech CEO and Its Impact on Scientific Research, WASH. POST (Sept. 23, 2013)*; see also *Neeley v. Wolters Kluwer Health, Inc.,*

No. 4:11-CV-325 JAR (E.D. Mo. July 29, 2013) (holding that publisher of drug risk manual can be liable to patients for publication of false information)

A scientist-CEO in a public press release to investment analysts touts his company's drug undergoing government regulatory approval as showing statistically significant success in treating the lung disease of a particular patient subset. The press release omits to mention that aggregate treatment data were statistically insignificant taken across all study populations, suggesting the drug's general invalidity. Furthermore, the particular 'responsive' subgroup highlighted in the press release was identified by retrospective analysis – a scientifically irregular or even unacceptable practice, commonly understood as such by fellow scientists, in which a subgroup showing positive response to the drug is identified only after the study is complete. If the press release does not identify that the subgroup was retrospectively identified, is the scientist-CEO's press release contextually tantamount to criminal fraud?

Whether courts will support regulators' punishments of corporate speech is unclear. Compare *Piazza's Seafood World, LLC v. Odom, 448 F.3d 744, 746, 753 (5th Cir. 2006)* with *Benson v. Kwikset Corp., 62 Cal. Rptr. 3d 284, 293, 295–95 (Cal. App. 2007)*

The United States Fifth Circuit struck down Louisiana's 'Cajun' statute, which defined all fish sold in Louisiana under the marking 'Cajun' to be catfish of Louisiana origin. Consequently, a company using the marking for fish imported from China that were a different species than domestic catfish was free to continue its use of the term 'Cajun'. The Fifth Circuit reasoned that because the importer was largely selling to wholesalers and clearly labelled the product's country of origin, there was little risk of actual deception and thus Louisiana's law was invalid as applied to the importer. By inexplicable contrast, a California appeals court deferred to a restrictive California statute that required any product sold in California and labelled 'Made in the USA' not only to be manufactured in the United States but to have its component parts manufactured in the United States.

The meaning of a corporation/union/organization's speech or activities can be hard to determine... but it will nevertheless be judged in court sometimes or even frequently... and that can be risky indeed!
San Antonio Cmty. Hosp. v. S. Cal. Dist. Council of Carpenters, 137 F.3d 1090, 1091 (9th Cir. 1998)

If a striking union pickets a hospital with signs that say, 'This hospital is full of rats!' is the proper proposition: 1) 'The hospital is a contractor that does not pay all of its employees prevailing wages or provide health and pension benefits to all of its employees'; or 2) 'The hospital has small furry rodents running rampant through it?'

Frigaliment Importing Co. v. B.N.S. International Sales Corp., 190 F. Sup. 116 (S.D.N.Y. 1960)

This famous 'chicken' case involved the legal issue of whether 'ordinary language'/'ordinary meaning' should be presumed as the default standard in contract matters. Of course, any student of Wittgenstein would protest that there is no ordinary meaning, that it is all contextual.

Garner v Burr[1951] 1 KB 31

The legislature had made it an offence to use a 'vehicle' on a road without pneumatic tyres. Lawrence Burr fitted iron wheels to his chicken coop, and pulled it down the road behind his tractor. Burr was prosecuted under the statute. The magistrates acquitted him, apparently on the ground that a chicken coop is not a 'vehicle'. The appeal court reversed that decision.

Pernod Ricard USA, LLC v. Bacardi U.S.A., Inc., 653 F.3d 241, 248–49 (3d Cir. 2011)

Is the brand name 'Havana Club' of a rum distilled in Puerto Rico equivalent to the proposition 'This rum was produced in Cuba'?

Buckley v. Littell, 539 F.2d 882, 893 (2d Cir. 1976) (finding that there is 'tremendous imprecision of the meaning and usage of these terms in the realm of political debate')

If someone is called a 'fascist' and 'radical right-winger,' what definition of those terms should be used to evaluate the plaintiff's claim of defamatory falsity?

> *McNeil-PPC, Inc. v. Pfizer Inc., 351 F. Supp. 2d 226, 231, 249–50 (S.D.N.Y. 2005)*

Does a television ad claiming 'Listerine is as effective as floss at fighting plaque and gingivitis. Clinical studies prove it' amount to the proposition that one need not floss if regularly using mouthwash?

> *Carter Prods., Inc. v. FTC, 323 F.2d 523, 526–28 (5th Cir. 1963)*

Is it a false product portrayal – amounting to the proposition 'This is exactly what your product will look like and how it will function' – if a mock-up of a shaving cream product is used in a television ad to portray comparative foaminess over other products if it would be otherwise impossible to show the actual benefits in the normal time allotted in a television ad?

> Context matters – sometimes very slight differences make all the difference in terms of legal risk. *McDermott v. Biddle, 674 A.2d 665, 665–66, 669 (Pa. 1996)*

Consider the curious Pennsylvania Supreme Court case in which the court upheld a jury's ruling that the same articles were true when printed in the *Philadelphia Inquirer* newspaper but false when reprinted in a tabloid.

Contract risk 06

Introduction

Let's be honest: contracts are a bit boring. To some they are a 'necessary evil' that add legal paper to the excitement of the deals they negotiate, and when the excitement of the deal is over, many companies refer to them (if they can find them) only when they are in commercial dispute, and rely instead on individual knowledge of deals to ensure commercial relationships stay on track. There are two reasons this is a bad idea.

First, contracts are a source of legal risk in themselves. Poorly-worded agreements can increase your liability, or open you up to regulatory sanction or class-action from angry customers. If you don't know what is in them, you don't know whether, or when, these risks will materialize. Secondly, contracts are a source of rich commercial information. They allocate risk between parties, define commercial reward and outline the legal remedies each party can take if they believe they aren't getting what they deserve. Good contracts are designed to influence specific commercial behaviours through financial incentives and penalties, and so avoid commercial dispute. If you do find yourself in dispute with a client or supplier, you will both rely on the contract as the single source of truth against which your behaviour will be judged. So use that contract proactively as a commercial management tool, and don't assume that your own behaviours will be judged to be acceptable regardless of what the contract may say. Prevention is better than cure, and if you want to prevent commercial disputes from draining profit and devaluing your company, you must pay attention to contractual risk.

You will read in this chapter about the most common risks associated with legal contract language, and also how measuring variance from standard terms can give you a good foundation to measure and manage contractual risk. Contractual risk is probably the best understood, most easily quantifiable and easiest to manage of our five risk categories, but the contract's most important role is as a risk management tool in its own right. For contracts to operate as an effective risk mitigant, they need to be managed throughout their lifecycle, with reference to the underlying risks. The foundation of contract risk management is an administrative task: knowing where your agreements are, knowing what's in them, and quantifying the risks and benefits that are right in front of you.

Why contracts matter

Contracts are integral to managing risk, driving efficiency in your business relationships, setting boundaries to collaboration inside and outside the organization, and managing costs through efficient practice and risk allocation. They are a core control, for example, for operational, credit and legal risk. If you use them as an active management tool, they set the foundation for the value of your business (imagine what your company would be worth if it had no written contracts) and, when used well, will increase your business value. If you include terms that discourage your business partners from working with you, leave contracts in your bottom drawer, or fail to enforce commercially beneficial rules, they can decrease your business value and in the worst possible scenario cause insolvency.

To illustrate how contracts are managed within companies, we have gathered a collection of contract risk 'war stories', all of which have been anonymized. Some have had huge financial and reputational implications, others are examples where good contract management has added real financial value to the business. The examples discuss the role contracts play in protecting your intellectual property, how enforcing negotiated payment terms can improve your working capital, and how bonus structures can add millions of dollars to your top line.

Example: contracts can (or should) protect your intellectual property

A senior manager in a product manufacturer came up with a brilliant idea that required a cooperation agreement with a consultancy company he had selected at random. Instead of working with the legal department to draft the agreement based on corporate standards, he used a template from his drawer. The drawer template was a software configuration consultancy agreement where all rights were vested in the other party instead of his company. If the senior manager had used the standard 'work for hire' template that the legal department would have provided, the company could have exploited the innovation. Instead the innovation was owned by the consultancy firm – which walked away – and many dollars were thrown down the drain. This is not the only example we have seen, and can be avoided if you enforce legal sign-off of non-approved contracts through robust contract governance structures.

Example: enforcing contracted payment terms can save working capital

One organization we know decided to compare payments against terms for its 150 highest spend suppliers. It discovered that on average it paid those suppliers 11 days early, and when it expanded the comparison to include the next 200 suppliers, the company found it paid suppliers on average 18 days early. By aligning the accounting systems with the actual negotiated contract payment terms, it improved net working capital by $24 million and $1.5 million in interest simply by paying on time (but not sooner). This is a great example of how contracts can be used to generate additional value, simply by knowing and acting on the negotiated terms.

Example: contracted incentive schemes can add to the top line

A similar example of the benefits of active contract management is to do with incentive schemes. During a contract management project one company noticed it had incentive schemes in some contracts but couldn't find any evidence that it had received all the bonuses agreed with the suppliers. To investigate, it initiated a small pilot analysis, with the objective of recovering any non-claimed applicable bonuses. It reviewed existing policies on incentive schemes, roles and responsibilities, and tested whether it actually received all bonuses. The pilot resulted in recovery of bonuses of more than half a million dollars and identification of future bonuses worth a potential $10 million dollars plus.

How to identify and manage contractual risk

So, contracts do matter. They are more than a 'necessary evil' that just add legal paper to a deal. But they also expose you to risk: through lack of awareness or poor management, you may fail to meet your obligations, enforce your rights or inadvertently waive rights through operational practices. To manage these risks you will need to engage a wide group of stakeholders to manage your contracts through their entire lifecycle. Later in this chapter we will review in detail the different stages of the contract lifecycle and the key risks you should manage at each stage.

Embedded within the contract is a wealth of legal language that acts as an incentive to particular behaviours. If the language is unclear, unfair or unenforceable in a court of law, it could lead to the wrong behaviour on either side. If your contracts miss core protections or wording required by regulators – regarding anti-bribery and corruption, for example – you could end up on the wrong side of a costly regulatory dispute or class-action type litigation. So to begin we will review how risk can be written into the contract, and outline a tool and examples of how this risk can be managed effectively.

Five core sources of risk in every contract

Life as an in-house lawyer is very different from that in private practice. In-house, legal support is allocated based on business risk and revenue, rather than the need to ensure that current legal theories are enshrined in your contracts. In-house teams learn to focus on what is important to the business's top and bottom line, and avoid the trap of thinking that 'everything is important'. Focusing on what is truly important in the contract is a key skill that takes time to learn. You need to balance commercial goals with legal certainty, and become comfortable with wording that isn't always 100 per cent in your favour.

Tools and techniques that shortcut the review process, without missing anything important, can dramatically improve contracting times. They consistently focus effort on a smaller number of contract 'data points' that give insight into a variety of priority risks, for example liability exposure across a suite of contracts, or the surprisingly common risk that business relationships aren't subject to a legally binding agreement. If you include unenforceable or unfair terms you may find yourself without legal protection in the event of a dispute, or if you are unclear about the terms you are agreeing to, you may not have the protections that you thought were there, or you may have agreed to receive services that don't match your expectation.

The checklist below details five common sources of risk you will find in almost any contract, and key things to look for in your own contract reviews. The checklist won't apply equally to all contracts, and you will need to adapt it to create contract-specific risk checklists for contracts where it makes sense to take a more consistent approach.

Checklist: Five sources of risk

1. Legal structure

The legal structure is the starting point for any contract and you should always review the contract to ensure the legal and structural integrity of the agreement is intact. For example:

- Is the correct type of template used and is the template fit for purpose?
- Is the contract signed by legal entities (and the right legal parties) and has the right signature block been adapted?

▶

- Does each party have authority to sign and create a binding agreement?
- Does the agreement contain inconsistencies? For example, check that the agreement has no cut-and-paste history.
- Make sure that the agreement links to the right exhibits or schedules (scope of work, price, technical descriptions, etc), and that language used in the exhibits or schedules flows into the agreement and isn't contradictory.

2. Your liability and commitments

You need to ensure that your company is prepared to assume the liability described in the contract. Examples are:

- Do not commit any other company in your group, or third parties, without their prior approval; and ensure you are able to meet your direct commitments under the contract.
- Do not accept unlimited liability. When you do cap your liability consider the overall value of the contractual arrangement to the other party, rather than simply capping it at the value of the contract.
- Do not accept liability for indirect losses or consequential damages.
- If you agree to cover for product liability or professional liability, for example, check it is covered by your insurance.
- Liquidated damages must be equitable and non-penal. Make sure that the liquidated damages are customized to the actual delivery or service provided. For example, if delivery is key within a short period, your liquidated damages percentage should be higher to create an incentive for the supplier to mitigate potential delay or failure to deliver. If the delivery or service is not critical, consider a lower percentage. If the context or purpose of your liquidated damages clause is open to misinterpretation, include explanatory wording in either the clause itself or the recitals to avoid potential future dispute.
- Ensure that warranties you make follow your corporate policies and are limited in time, scope and remedies available. For the customer it's equally important that the warranties negotiated are warranties that the supplier actually can deliver – and at the same time give you sufficient cover.

3. Your rights

You must ensure that the plan outcome is solidly described and supported by contract clauses and that your rights are protected within the contract. This is how you use the contract to influence the other side to give you what you expect. Here are some examples:

- Take a commercial view of the risks associated with transfer of rights. For example, as a supplier you may not want to accept any transfer or assignment of rights (intellectual property, for instance) except for the right to use the product/service 'as intended'. On the other hand, you may argue as a customer that you should always secure a right to use and have protection for infringement through an indemnity. If the product/service is specifically developed and paid for by the customer, it should also include a full transfer of IP rights. As the customer you should always secure a right to use.
- Ensure that there is a change of control clause in material agreements.
- Ensure that the scope is described and that 'change of control' clauses protect you when changes occur.
- Set out clearly the circumstances in which you can walk away from the contract.

4. Commerciality

All contracts must undergo a value vs risk review. You should review the value and strategic importance of the contractual arrangement to your business. This ties into your relationship management approach, as the categorization of your suppliers/customers might become the indicator for the levels between risk/value.

- Confirm that the commercial terms are acceptable for the level of risk represented in the contract, and for the ongoing relationship it creates.
- Ensure that the importance of the contract to your business continuity is reflected in the terms, and that an adequate fall-back plan is in place.
- Secure ongoing performance reviews and sufficient pricing mechanics.

5. Regulatory and policy requirements

Check for provisions that require third parties to adhere to regulations that affect your business or your own internal policies. Confirm that required regulatory provisions are included, such as those that relate to:

- anti-bribery and corruption;
- corporate sustainability requirements;
- data protection;
- health and safety requirements;
- environmental protection requirements;
- intellectual property;
- anti-competitive behaviour.

Example: risk analysis in commercial insurance agreements

Commercial insurance coverage is one area of contract-specific risk that affects all commercial enterprises. If your coverage isn't what you believe it to be, you may take on risk that you haven't accounted for in either the price of the contract or the capital you set aside to cover the risk. This gap could expose your business to unexpected financial losses. This is particularly relevant from a risk management perspective, because risks that are not insured commercially are typically self-insured, for example through the holding of additional operating capital. Risk assessments of business operation, how profit is generated, potential liabilities and other risks (including legal risk) can help management to manage and transfer risk efficiently. They are a good first step to determine which risks should be covered by a third party, and those that should be covered through self-insurance.

Even when you have taken out commercial insurance to cover a set of risks, it can be difficult to identify exactly which circumstances you're insured for, which losses are covered and which are not. The box below defines a set of risks that are specific to insurance agreements, as a way of determining potential gaps in coverage and avoiding future disputes. This is essentially a review to check that you have the rights you expect and so validate the commerciality of the deal. This sort of review, carried out systematically over all your commercial insurance policies, could influence renewal fees and help ensure that your coverage meets your expectations.

Sources of risk in commercial insurance agreements

Coverage gaps

- *Unanticipated losses.* It isn't always possible to foresee all potential forms of loss when your insurance coverage is bound. Typically the more experienced the business, the better it will be able to 'look into the future' to determine risks it needs to insure against. Even then you will sometimes find outlier exposures that weren't contemplated by management.
- *Missing items.* Gaps in coverage occur when there is an oversight in what should be listed in the policy. For example, your policy might list specific property, rather than have general language to cover all property. You may have failed to list additional items in the policy.
- *Coverage amounts.* For example, it's necessary to maintain the proper underlying coverage aggregate limits under an umbrella policy. A gap can occur either if the underlying policy language is different to the umbrella policy terms, or the actual limits are lower than those required by the umbrella.
- *Definitions.* Definitions can limit losses under a policy too. What you thought of as a covered loss may not actually be defined as such under the policy. Reading the defined terms in the policy will determine the meaning of language used in the contract.
- *Interpretations.* Your interpretation of a term or condition in the policy may be different from that of the insurer. For example, a term that is defined as 'sales' may be calculated differently by the insured and insurer.

Exclusions

- *Ambiguous language.* It's important to know the policy exclusions. Considering a general liability policy, for example, typically the language seems to begin by covering a broad range of losses but actually provides exceptions in certain instances through exclusions. For example, if you are a growing enterprise, you may find that as you acquire companies, or enter into joint ventures, the acts of the other companies may be excluded under the commercial policy.

- *Defence of lawsuits.* Another example of exclusions involves the defence of a lawsuit by the insurance company. Some contracts may state the insurer has the right, but not the obligation, to defend the litigation, while other policies contain terms to which party defence costs are allocated. There are also policies where the defence costs of litigation serve as a deductible. How these costs will impact the actual cost of coverage can and should be considered when the policy is bound.
- *Conditions.* Conditions can set a limit to losses that are covered under a specific policy, or a loss threshold below which losses won't be paid. For example, an umbrella policy typically requires that underlying coverage be in place and used before losses under the umbrella are paid out.

Period of validity

- *Claims-made policies.* Claims-made policies cover losses that both occur and are submitted, or 'made', during the time period while the policy is in force. A claims-made policy that is no longer in force cannot be used for coverage even if the loss occurred while you were insured. Adverse situations may arise when an insured company changes carriers or binds new coverage. Losses may have already occurred but have not yet come to the attention of the insured. Insured companies may consider purchasing 'prior acts' supplemental coverage to cover potential claims that occurred as a result of past company actions.
- *Claims-occurrence policies.* A claims-occurrence policy will cover the losses that occur only during the period of coverage. It therefore is inconsequential whether or not the policy is still outstanding when the claim is submitted. Recognizing whether your policy is a claims-made or claims-occurrence policy will help protect the company, especially when shopping for replacement coverage or lower rates.

Contracts and proactive dispute risk management

The International Association for the Commercial and Contract Management conducts annual research that compares the most negotiated contract terms with the terms that are most important to success of the supplier-customer relationship. In the 2013/14 survey (IACCM, 2016) only six of the top 10 most negotiated terms matched the list of top 10 terms that were most important to the success of the relationship; see Table 6.1.

Table 6.1 Comparison of most negotiated versus most important terms, 2013/14

	Most negotiated terms	Most important terms
1	Limitation of liability	Scope and goals
2	Price/charge/price changes	Responsibilities of the parties
3	Indemnification	Change management
4	Service levels and warranties	Delivery/acceptance
5	Payment	Communications and reporting
6	Service withdrawal/termination	Price/charge/price changes
7	Warranty	Service levels and warranties
8	Intellectual property	Performance/guarantees/undertakings
9	Performance/guarantees/undertakings	Payment
10	Delivery/acceptance	Limitation of liability

SOURCE: www2.iaccm.com, 2016

It is beyond question that your legal team should focus on the terms that are most important to the success of your relationship, but not all relationships run smoothly. If your termination clauses and entire agreement clauses are clear and effective, or the purpose of the contract is clearly set out in the recitals, hopefully you won't get into a dispute in the first place. These aren't things you can change once you're in a dispute: if you get them wrong you could see valuable time and money being spent on disputes that could (and should) have been avoided!

Governing law and jurisdiction

The two most important clauses in international contracts, from a dispute perspective, are governing law and jurisdiction. If you're in the wrong courts or under the wrong law you may be sunk before you start. You can go a long way to avoiding a jurisdiction battle by addressing this properly in your contract. If you've already agreed to the exclusive jurisdiction of the courts in a particular territory, there's little or nothing even the most talented litigators can do about it.

Termination clauses

If it's easy for your supplier to walk away your business could get into trouble. How easily can you terminate and how clear are the provisions allowing you to do so? If you try to terminate a contract when you don't have a right to do so, you might inadvertently put yourself in repudiatory breach and give the other side the right to terminate and claim damages if it wants to.

Exclusion, entire agreement clauses and recitals

What about the effectiveness or otherwise of exclusion clauses and entire agreement clauses? Have you successfully prevented the other party later asserting that the agreement was part oral/part written, or that it relied on a pre-contractual misrepresentation when entering into the contract? Don't ignore the importance of recitals: they can provide valuable context for contracts that makes it much harder for a party to misconstrue other parties' intentions later.

Understanding where the sources of risk are in your contract, and mitigating them during contract review, is an important first step to improving contract risk management in your organization. Tools like the 'Five sources of risk' checklist can save lawyer time, as well as improving consistency throughout your contractual estate. The next step to good contract risk management is to begin to aggregate the risk data within and across contract types to identify where risk is pooling and spot outliers in your contractual estate that require remediation.

How to measure contract risk in terms of variance from standard terms

You don't need to have the best templates, the most elegant drafters, or the most brilliant lawyers to quantify and monitor contract risk (although they do help!). You simply need to measure the value that your contracts capture, and the risks that they distribute. Risk is typically measured in terms of an acceptable level of variance within an agreed threshold. In Chapter 3 we discussed that threshold as being an acceptable level of financial loss. When we apply that principle to contract risk, we set a threshold in terms of agreed negotiating positions from standard terms, and measure risk in terms of variance within those negotiation thresholds.

Your standard terms are most commonly captured in a 'standard document' or 'precedent'. A 'standard document' sets out the terms you will accept as standard and may contain aggressive variations and minimum acceptable terms. For example, it will contain your preferred and acceptable positions on the legal jurisdiction that will take precedence in the event of dispute, and the acceptable commercial aspects of the deal. A precedent is a document that has been previously approved and so may be used as a foundation for accepting or rejecting certain terms.

Unfortunately, whether or not your suppliers or customers agree to your standard terms is a combination of their bargaining power and ability/desire to pay the costs associated with negotiation. You can't always guarantee that your standard terms will be accepted by the other side, but even so, developing a good set of standard documentation, in partnership with your commercial teams, will result in documents that your commercial teams understand, reduced negotiation time and possibly a decrease in overall legal risk. They will also provide a foundation for implementing technology or alternative sourcing solutions to extract and report key terms from pre- or post-executed contracts, and report them in contract risk dashboards for management review.

There are tools based on a new generation of artificial intelligence that convert contracts into structure data and measure variance in key contractual 'hot-spots'. Their application can save thousands of hours of lawyer time, and give a level of oversight of contract risk that will bring comfort to many General Counsel (GC). Similarly, standardizing and codifying your standard documents and negotiating positions make it possible to use lower cost legal resource, such as contract lawyers or Legal Process Outsourcers (LPOs) with a greater degree of confidence that they will be able to work consistently within your guidelines, without constantly referring exceptions back to your in-house legal team. Selecting where to apply this kind of outsourcing or automation relies largely on your ability to categorize your contracts into one of three types: entirely standard, largely standard and heavily negotiated.

From a risk perspective, there are (arguably) only three types of contract: entirely standard, largely standard and heavily negotiated.

1. Entirely standard

Contracts based entirely on standard terms that require no negotiation, for example credit card or mobile phone terms and conditions. From a risk perspective you are interested in the sum total value and volume of all contracts of a particular type and the impact of changes to the legal or market position on the contractual relationship; and the ability to manage changes to terms and conditions when required.

2. Largely standard

Contracts with commercial terms that are usually negotiated, but based on a standard legal template, often with predefined negotiating positions. For example, corporate loan facilities, franchise agreements or OTC derivatives contracts. For largely standard agreements, from a risk perspective you want to measure value, volume and impact of changes to the legal or market position (as above) to the basic standard text, plus variations in commercial terms and technical language.

Note: Because standard and largely standard documents form the foundation of a huge portion of your contractual estate, it is worth having them drafted by the best commercial legal team you can find, to minimize the inherent risk. You might only be drafting a £20,000 agreement, but if you negotiate 2,000 of them each year, your risk multiple is £40 million!

3. Heavily negotiated (at first glance, bespoke)

For heavily negotiated, typically high-value/high complexity agreements (for example, complex material outsourcing agreements, master supply agreements, or complex partnership agreements) your first line of defence is the legal team. To double-check negotiating positions across a variety of agreements, identify and analyse key clauses that control your commercial and legal risks (see above), and compare the individual clause to acceptable/industry standard wording. This approach enables you to pinpoint the most material risks, measure the level of variance against preferred terms/wording, and evaluate the effect of the external environment on those terms.

Contract analytics technology, and use of LPOs and contract lawyers is developing quickly, but they rely on your legal experts to tell them what is important in the contract, and in your commercial experts to price additional risk into the commercial terms.

Contracts as a key risk management tool

Contracts are by their nature a risk management mechanism. They set out the expected outcome of a business relationship, the recourse you have if you don't get what you expect, and what will happen if you don't deliver your side of the deal. Correctly drafted (and communicated) the contract will articulate the business relationship and act as an operational handbook to govern the relationship from initial order to dispute resolution. As you read in the previous section, key terms on liability, guarantees and step-in rights, for example, can act as core risk mitigants – provided they are clearly communicated and each party does their best to stick to them. The next case study outlines how global protective services company, Securitas, has put contracts at the heart of its risk management activity. Despite evidence of contracts' potential for use as an operational risk management tool, as demonstrated in this case, operational risk professionals rarely seem to recognize the contract as a core risk control document.

CASE STUDY Securitas put contracts at the centre of its risk management strategy

Securitas is a global protective services company that put contract risk management at the heart of its risk evaluation matrix. It is a great example of a company that treats contracts as a core risk control. From its 2009 annual report onwards, Securitas provided details of its business risk evaluation model, 'The scale'. The model contains four stages: Assignment, Risk, Contract and Financials.

Assignment: How well scoped is the service, has it been carried out before and what are the set-up and delivery costs?

Risk: Is the customer high risk, or are there any assignment-specific risks that can be managed proactively – for example, install CCTV cameras to reduce theft?

Contract: 'A fair division of responsibilities and risks between Securitas and the customer is essential in every contract. Standardized contracts are the norm. Reasonable caps on potential liability and indemnification for third-party claims are important.' (Securitas Annual Report, 2009)

Financials: Overall profitability of the business, to include assessment of off-balance sheet exposure in the contract, and payment terms.

The contract lifecycle

All contracts follow a similar lifecycle that divides across the point in time where the contract is executed. All activities that take place pre-contract are designed to make sure you get the best deal from a tactical and strategic perspective. A large portion of your efforts to limit the risks that sit within the contract will take place in this phase: ensuring that you have the right template, understanding the key commercial aspects of the deal, for example, and ensuring the right legal language is used to avoid future regulatory issues. When you have concluded negotiations, check that you are executing with approved signatories on each side to ensure you have a binding agreement.

All activities after the contract is signed have one purpose: to ensure that you receive the anticipated value. Normally it would be delivery with a satisfied customer (on time, price and quality) or ensuring that the deliverables are met. In this delivery phase, contracts are often forgotten in favour of a business-as-usual approach to the engagement. The majority of contract disputes happen when this approach leads one party to feel it isn't getting the value it expected from the deal.

Figure 6.1 outlines a typical contract lifecycle that can be applied to a huge variety of contracts. It outlines seven stages of the lifecycle, which are then explained in detail in the following text. The narrative makes reference to supply-side contract negotiations, and is peppered with real-life examples of what can happen if any point of the lifecycle is mismanaged.

Figure 6.1 Typical contract lifecycle

1. Set goals

The first step of any contract negotiation is to identify the stakeholders who want to create the contractual relationship, meet with them to confirm scope, targets and schedule, and work through an initial project plan that will deliver their agreed commercial goals. Failure to define commercial goals and success factors can result in a poor negotiation strategy that will destroy your deal value. This initial process will also ensure that you have the required authority to begin negotiations.

Example: Negotiating without authority can cost you your job

A marketing manager spent a year negotiating a €200,000 contract, and used up a lot of legal and finance department time and resource. At no point in the process did she secure internal approval for the contract to ensure execution. The company was not prepared to spend €200,000 on a marketing campaign. The deal didn't get signed, and the marketing manager was asked to leave the company.

Another person in sourcing did even worse. He decided to enter into a sponsorship agreement with a local sports club. The agreement was negotiated and signed, and even presented at a press conference before the company identified that the individual wasn't 'authorized to sign'. He had no authority to enter into a binding agreement, so the agreement was declared void, his employment was terminated, and the local sports club did not see the money.

2. *Negotiation*

After you have defined your commercial goals, collect data that will inform the negotiation and help you to develop and execute a strategy that gives you the best chance of achieving those goals. If you have a previous relationship with a supplier, for example, you will have commercial data that will inform the negotiation. You may be able to review spend/volume/revenue forecasts and create a baseline for a Total Cost of Ownership (TCO) or Total Value of Ownership (TVO) model. When you have all the data to hand, think about holding an internal brainstorming or idea generation meeting with all stakeholders to develop ideas you can test later against market data.

When you have developed your strategy, prepare and issue a Request for Information (RFI) that sets out performance criteria you can use to qualify and rank the supplier base, and Key Performance Indicators (KPIs) that can be used to monitor future performance. After receiving your RFI, map the responses and compare them with industry best practice to formulate a specific sourcing strategy, as well as supplier selection criteria. Then prepare and issue a Request for Proposal (RFP) that sets the basis for future contract negotiation, assesses the suppliers/partners, and ensures they are willing to comply with your internal policies and regulatory requirements. Following a formal process will not only ensure that you get what you are looking for from the negotiation, but also that you have the authority to negotiate on behalf of your company.

Because they also feed into the commercial delivery of the deal, the five sources of risk checklist we detailed earlier is a valuable tool to help keep negotiations on track and to avoid otherwise preventable legal risks.

Example: Contracts can make or destroy your margins

In early 2010 a software company advised on a turnkey project. No one had defined clearly how the company would recognize revenue during the project. Before the negotiations began, on paper the margins looked great. But throughout negotiations the customer pushed for a very strong final acceptance procedure, and backed this up with strong legal wording in the contract. Despite great margins, the unanticipated costs associated with meeting the acceptance procedures meant huge revenue losses as time went by.

3. *Execution*

Assuming you have authority to sign the agreement, follow your company standard processes for signing and execution. For strategic contracts, create a summary and/or contract operational guide, and ensure the contract is included in requirements for performance reporting. Then make sure that the contract is stored securely – preferably in searchable electronic form – so that it can be retrieved later.

Example: Asking suppliers for their copy of your contract is at best embarrassing

An in-house lawyer started her first job as General Counsel for a global electronics company. Part of her role was to ensure the company had agreements in place for key services. She started from a low base and the project took several years. During this time she came across several instances where she could not retrieve hard copies (or even soft copies in draft) of old agreements, and had to call suppliers to ask them for a copy. This was embarrassing, but real trouble arose when she was preparing for a multi-million dollar law suit and could not locate a signed version of the agreement. The company ended up in a situation where it was questioning whether it had a binding agreement against which it could sue.

4. Contract deployment

After selecting a supplier/partner, you need to establish a plan to communicate the new relationship to all internal stakeholders, as well as those on the other side. Key stakeholders need to know that the agreement has been finalized, and what the core obligations and rights are for each party. Prepare a handover note for delivery units that includes the services/performance levels that have been agreed and upload financial numbers and prices into your procurement systems.

This is also the right time to begin a process to optimize payment terms and payment flow (where possible) and to make sure the incentive structures (financial or non-financial) relate clearly to desired outcomes and are well managed and governed with appropriate checks and approval mechanisms. This is also a good time to ensure that roles and responsibilities are clear and clearly allocated. It is great to be part of a team that creates well prepared, nicely negotiated agreements with appropriate terms and conditions in place, but this will be of limited benefit to you if the contract owner doesn't deploy the contract into the organization and hand it over to the operational implementation team. When that happens, you will generally fail to deliver on time, quality and scope, and have to deal with furious senior management and – even worse – a really angry customer. You need to get your legal department to give clear guidance to contracting staff (whether on the sales or supply side of the business) on how to manage and operate contractual commitments post-signature, how to ensure they don't enter into a binding agreement by mistake, and how to avoid amending or waiving legally binding contractual terms inadvertently.

5. Manage performance

If you have set performance criteria in the negotiation stage, you will be well placed to monitor supplier or client performance from the moment the contract is deployed within the business. You monitor service levels and KPIs for contracts to ensure there is a continuous link to operational needs (strategic suppliers) and ongoing monitoring of compliance with contractual 'non-performance issues', for example anti-corruption and export control.

Use supplier scorecards, based on KPIs, to give regular feedback (formal and informal) to the responsible category manager on the supplier/client performance (paying on time, etc). Another aspect of performance management is to check that operational compliance measurements (price models, operational use of contracts, etc) are in place and being followed. Again, ensure business units are aware of deployed contracts and have a schedule in place to carry out contract audit checks (invoice, performance, delivery, quality, bonuses). Even if you sign outsourcing contracts with a well-respected firm, the performance of the outsourcing still needs to be managed and monitored as part of your standard operating practices.

Example: You can't rely on a single individual's knowledge of the deal

One client signed up to an outsourcing deal with over 4,000 line items. To manage contract performance he relied on an individual who had been involved in the contract negotiation from the beginning and knew the deal 'inside-out'. Unfortunately for him, that individual left the company to join the supplier, leaving him with a huge knowledge gap and no way to adequately manage the outsourcing without employing external counsel to review and summarize the contract.

6. Contract development

Implement a process to review and update contracts regularly. Also put in place a process to manage the relationship outside of the contractual terms, to ensure the relationship continues to meet the evolving needs of your business and represents continued value for money. As part of your supplier relationship management, agree resolution processes to ensure minor problems do not escalate and cause relationship issues. You might implement a relationship charter, for example, to avoid a blame culture developing between your business teams and your suppliers. You might also implement a process to capture innovation from the supplier, and set overall objectives for the supplier relationship beyond the individual contract.

Any changes to requirements should be handled through a proper and efficient contractual change approval flow, to ensure you don't inadvertently amend or waive your contractual rights, and be documented and communicated to ensure you have a record of the amendments. It is common, for example, for business units to implement operational changes or accept side-terms by e-mail that amend or waive contractual terms. When this is done without reference to the original contract, or to the legal department, it opens you up to potential legal dispute if the commercial aspects of the deal go awry.

Example: Amendments to terms need to be written down and communicated

A global commodities conglomerate had a commonly used structure with frame agreements and a process where price fluctuations were documented outside of the frame in a 'living document'. Price fluctuations were volatile and could make or break the organization's financial quarter. In one quarter, procurement agreed new fixed prices with the supplier and reported back to management. A change in the market led to what would have been a price increase of 100 per cent the next week. The procurement team were really happy until they realized they had no evidence for the agreed price change – and the supplier denied all knowledge of the negotiation. To be fair to the procurement team, very few suppliers would let their customers take a hit like this and risk the future business relationship: in this case the supplier took that risk.

7. Renewal (or termination)

Renewal (or termination) is an important part of the lifecycle that too often gets left to the last minute. Identify and prioritize renegotiations and create a renewal pipeline based on expiry dates and performance monitoring. To improve efficiency, measure the average time it takes to process each type of contract and pass what is learnt from each negotiation forward to the next. You will eventually be able to use this type of data to measure the efficiency of your standard contracts, adjust legal support to meet known peaks in demand, and match risk levels to business need. Most importantly of all, don't leave contracts to run indefinitely without review and renewal. You can't, as you will read in the next chapter, rely on the courts to get you out of a long-standing deal that no longer makes the same commercial sense it did when you originally signed it.

Example: Contract law changes, so review contracts regularly

Having a contract with no end-date may require less effort with renegotiation, but it exposes you to greater risk than having to negotiate or extend the contract every X number of years. One lawyer found that it was standard practice in her organization to 'evergreen' contracts, ie deliberately have no end-date to a business relationship. Some relationships had been running for tens of years without a review of contractual terms. If this relationship broke down, it is possible – and in the UK probable – that you will be held to the terms in the original contract, whether or not they make commercial sense. The lawyer in question implemented a programme to systematically review all evergreen contracts. In two years she had eliminated the legal risk and negotiated improved terms into many of the agreements.

How to improve contracting practice in your organization

The harsh truth is that a lot of companies still don't know where they keep their contracts and what obligations and rights are contained within them. There are some companies that have begun a journey to move contracts out of the 'bottom drawer' and into digital management systems, but of those who are on that journey, the majority are taking their first steps.

Five stakeholder groups typically have overlapping interests in contracts

One of the barriers to good contracting practices is the number of internal groups that have a stake in negotiation and delivery of the contract. If you have ever managed any kind of project you will know that the more stakeholders you have, the less likely you are to deliver on time and on budget. Stakeholders have different and often conflicting views and the same is true of the contracting process. There are typically five key stakeholder groups (see Figure 6.2): legal, commercial teams (for example, credit teams), operations, negotiation teams (for example, purchasing, sales, HR) and finance, whose views on what is important need to be kept in balance.

Figure 6.2 Contract management stakeholders

We put lawyers at the centre of this group of stakeholders because they understand the technicalities of the contract, and have a good sight of each of the different stakeholders' points of view. There is a real opportunity for GC and their legal departments to take responsibility for the contract throughout its entire lifecycle. This level of operational involvement is outside the comfort zone of many legal departments, and it will involve more accountability for administration and business processes across parts of the business that they have previously been insulated from.

However, it is important to make the distinction that while legal teams should be involved in the design of contract management processes, and have oversight of the activities that involve contracts at all points of their lifecycle, they shouldn't necessarily own the delivery of the whole process. Legal departments will often take the blame for contract failures even when they are the result of operational failings that are outside their control. So if they take a more emphatic supervisory role across the contract lifecycle, they can reduce the operational failings that result in legal loss, analyse the unrealized value that is embedded in the contractual estate, play a central role in increasing the overall value of the business, and increase their standing in the organization.

The matrix shown in Figure 6.3 will give you an idea of where to allocate responsibility for different contract management tasks. The matrix divides the work of the legal department into four quadrants, and different tasks related to contract management are allocated across each of the quadrants. The matrix includes some non-contractual tasks, to add perspective. If you are a GC, you can use the matrix to decide which types of work should sit in the business or be automated (bottom left), which can be automated or pushed externally with the right level of supervision (bottom right and top left), and which should be owned specifically by you (top right). To use this yourself, review the risk and value associated with your legal department's activities, and the importance of each activity to your business, to place them in one of the four quadrants. Then take a strategic view as to whether you want them to be delivered externally or internally, and what an appropriate level of supervision looks like. This kind of strategic approach is essential to avoid unnecessary – and possibly

Figure 6.3 Legal work priority matrix

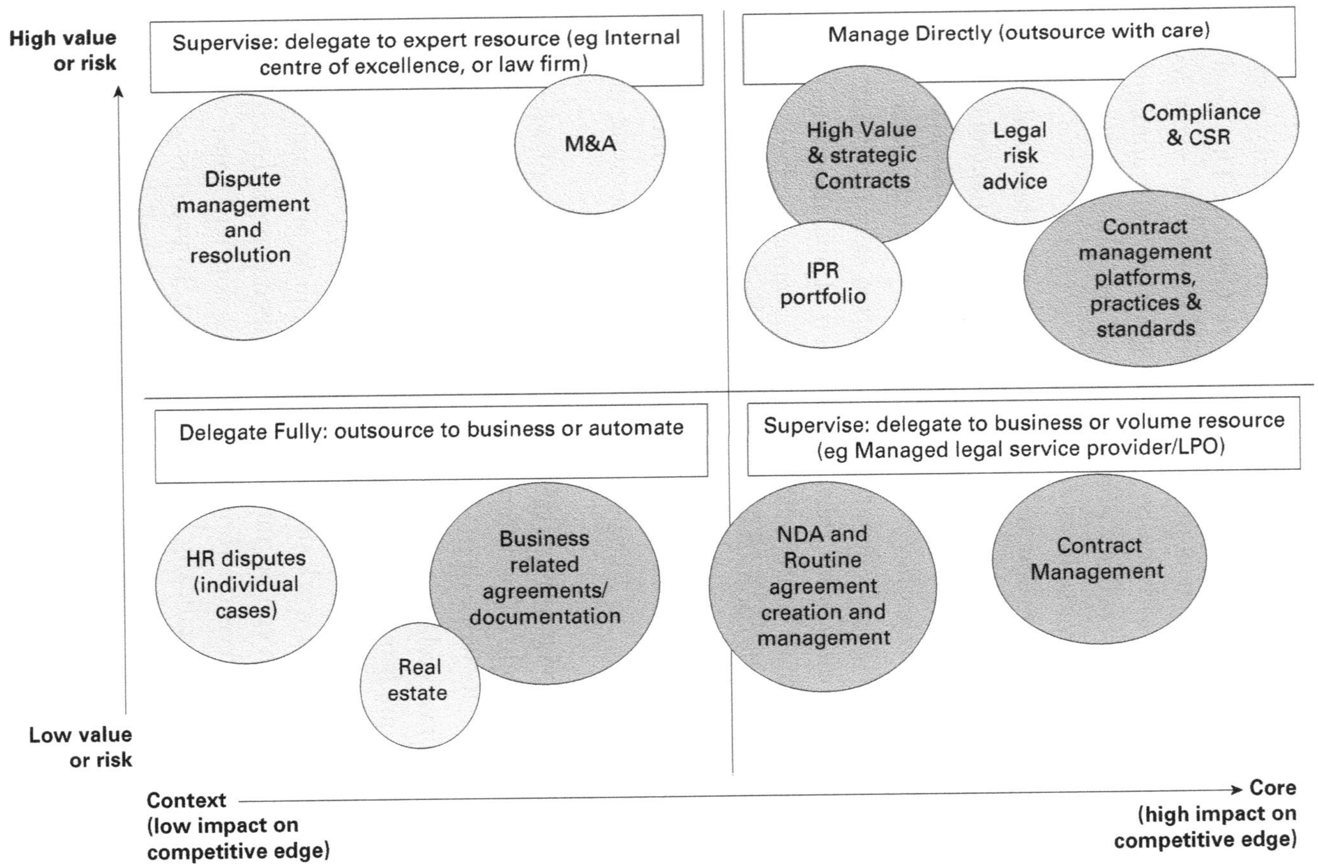

SOURCE: Adapted with permission from CBI Contract Intelligence

wasteful – use of expensive lawyer time. More important, it enables you to leverage the knowledge of your legal department to deliver insight to the business in terms of legal risk management and potential business opportunity.

For GC there is an opportunity to outsource the mundane aspects of contract drafting and standardized negotiation, either externally or to the business, and to design platforms that gather risk data that gives insight across a broad range of business activities. Once freed from the day-to-day tasks in the bottom-left and bottom-right quadrants, in-house lawyers can focus on strategic advisory issues in the top-right and closer supervision of activities in the top-left quadrant. They can advise the business how to manage legal risk in its other forms, and how contract data can be used to identify opportunities to generate greater profits, or reduce risk exposure and therefore risk capital.

Prioritize high-value contracts and reduce high-volume costs

If you do take ownership of contracts as a GC, take a risk-based perspective to decide which contracts should be tracked on a company-wide basis, then set policies and procedures to use contract data to mitigate the risks within those contracts. When you have a good view of all the contracts in your business, you can review current contracting processes to identify potential efficiency savings and pinpoint data embedded within your contracts that will help flag potential legal and operational risks.

CASE STUDY Simplifying NDAs to save cost and reduce risk

A global trade shipping and energy conglomerate conducted an exercise to simplify its Non-disclosure Agreements (NDAs). NDAs are a very common form of legal agreement that impose confidentiality requirements on individuals or companies. This company processed around 5,000 per year, but had never been party to an NDA dispute. The risk – how confidential information was treated by third parties – wasn't dealt with through the standard non-disclosure language. The company also often negotiated multiple NDAs with the same third party. Following an exercise to identify different risk categories, standardize contract language and build a simple contract template, the company moved from a position where it created and signed 5,000 NDAs per year to 250 per year. If you calculate the time savings using a conservative three hours per contract in processing time, it moved 15,000 hours of work out of the organization. As a follow-up exercise it made significant text reductions to other templates to make them more user-friendly and generate even more efficiencies.

This requires as a start that you have knowledge of contracts you have entered into and, as a next step, in-depth knowledge of each and every item in the contracts. If legal are to take a central role, they need to encourage a change in mind-set across stakeholder groups about how a contract develops and is passed around the organization throughout its life. When your contract stakeholders all have the same view of the contract lifecycle, they can coordinate resources to reduce the negotiation cycle and share knowledge to create a shared technical and commercial understanding of what the contracts mean to day-to-day business operations and value.

Options to resource contract management

If you decided to follow through with any of the suggestions in this chapter, you are going to need to increase, or rethink, the resources you allocate to contract management. We have touched briefly on how AI-based technology and low-cost resourcing models can be deployed to reduce the costs associated with effective contractual risk management, and we've looked at a strategic model to assess which tasks should be allocated internally, externally or kept within the legal department.

New entrants have arrived in the legal market in the wake of improved knowledge of how legal work can be disaggregated and distributed to skilled resource pools, depending on its complexity.

This has come at an opportune moment for in-house legal teams. Because they need to take a more strategic advisory role with their business, and at the same time manage costs more efficiently, they are increasingly willing to give work to LPOs, contract lawyers, and managed legal service providers.

Using LPOs and contract lawyer resource has enabled in-house teams to move up the value chain by taking on low-value low-impact work from large clients. Some law firms have reacted by setting up low-cost centres and offering lower cost managed legal services of their own. For example, Allen & Overy LLP, one of the UK's 'magic circle' firms and a leading international law firm, set up one of the first teams of legal professionals based in Belfast in 2011, and in 2013 set up its own contract lawyer service, 'Peerpoint'.

At the same time, standardizing approaches and improved technology are enabling supervised contract management teams to move across the value chart and increase the complexity of work they deal with. Contract analytics and contract robots provide another option in lower-complexity work, and also have potential to expand across the value chain as they improve. Taken collectively, these new resource pools and technology options, combined with traditional law firm services, increase the options available to businesses to allocate legal services externally, without losing control of risk management.

Summary

Contracts expose you to risk in two ways. First, they could be poorly drafted. They may be missing key legal terms required by regulators, or fail to incorporate legal protections that you mistakenly rely on to reduce your risk. You can mitigate these risks by allocating central responsibility for contract risk management to your legal department, implementing tools and technology to standardize your negotiating and risk thresholds as much as is commercially practical, and employing alternative resources and technology to supplement the contract negotiation and review process, and systematically manage and report contractual risk.

The second way that contracts expose you to risk is through underuse. Contracts act as a risk mitigation tool, and contain a rich vein of commercial data that you can use to reduce risk and maximize value from your existing contractual relationships. However, it is common practice to ignore contracts as a management tool, and refer to them only when you are subject to some form of commercial dispute. There are reasons for this: multiple stakeholders have different views of what is important, and so no one takes ownership. Contents of contracts aren't always communicated to implementation teams by the lawyers, so they are forgotten in favour of individual knowledge of deals. A lack of resource across the organization to implement core operational improvements can make it difficult for legal teams to make the improvements they know are needed.

These issues are all surmountable. New resourcing options, such as LPOs, contract lawyers and legal managed services have decreased the costs associated with negotiating and reviewing contracts. New technology is becoming available that will enable businesses to digitize risk-based contract reviews, and report risks within the individual contract and across all contracts within specific categories. These technologies distil contracts into three buckets – standard, largely standard and bespoke – and are slowly leading to increased standardization across contract types.

Prevention is better than cure, so perhaps the most important area of contractual risk management is in proactively managing the contract throughout its lifecycle. When it is taken out of the 'bottom drawer' and used as a proactive commercial and risk management tool, issues will be exposed earlier, risk mitigation actions can be planned in advance, and business risks can be reduced to a series of known potential events that can be offset with commercial insurance products. This will enable businesses to focus on how to extract value from the rich commercial data currently locked within their contracts.

Dispute risk 07

I constantly am amazed at how often in-house counsel (and Compliance personnel) defer to outside counsel about litigation strategy and staffing. (Mel Schwarz)

Introduction

Prevention is better than cure. However, if your legal risk mitigation efforts fail across any of the legislative/regulatory, non-contractual obligations, non-contractual rights or contractual risk categories, you are likely to find yourself in some form of legal dispute and in need of the advice contained in this chapter.

Legal disputes create a direct link between underlying legal risks and financial loss. When you pay for legal advice in relation to litigation, or make provisions against projected litigation in your accounts, you put a direct financial loss against the root legal risk. In the first chapter we reviewed four charts (Figure 1.1), that plotted litigation costs and expenses for four US banks between 2010 and 2014. The charts showed a total financial cost to those banks of over $23 billion over that five-year period. Not all sectors are as litigious as banking, and that period of time post-crisis was particularly fraught in that sector, but dispute risk management is something for which you need a strategy.

It is worth reiterating here that 'dispute risk' is the risk that you will mismanage some part of the dispute process either in the run-up to the dispute, or during the dispute itself, which will somehow increase your quantum of loss. Because the vast majority (95 per cent) of disputes never go to trial, the decisions you make, or that are made on your behalf by external law firms, will directly impact costs and settlement figures. We estimate that if you follow the right strategy, maintain control of information flow as much as possible, and stick to the formal court timelines, you can reduce your loss – or increase your gain – by up to 30 per cent. When billions of dollars could be at stake, 30 per cent is a career-enhancing margin.

The reality of dispute management is nuanced, and it is tempting to simply instruct external counsel and let them get on with the case. In fact this area of legal risk management is almost always outsourced to external counsel, but if you have a good knowledge of the process and the key factors that litigators consider, you can influence and give support to external counsel that will speed up the process, greatly reduce your costs, and ultimately increase your prospects of success either at trial or through a favourable settlement. If you take this option, you must ask yourself several questions: How strong is my documentary, witness and expert evidence likely to be? Is the law on my side? How reliable are the courts in the jurisdiction where I'm going to be litigating? How much is it all going to cost? What are my chances of getting my money back even if I win?

These are just some of the questions that a good litigator has at the front of his or her mind right from the start of any dispute. Litigation is time-consuming, expensive and can have damaging reputational consequences if you get it wrong. If you have a clear strategy in your approach to disputes and remember the key factors that influence litigation success you will be able to make the right strategic decisions on which cases to pursue, and where to prioritize your litigation spending.

This chapter acts as a guide to non-litigators (whether lawyers or not) who have oversight of almost any kind of dispute. It will help you to get an accurate picture of the merits of each case, contains tools to help you derive a mathematical assessment of your likelihood of success, gives best practice approaches to enforcement to maximize your chances of receiving your award, and discusses litigation finance options that can take the cost of fighting disputes off your balance sheet.

When to start managing dispute risk

Dispute risk management begins the moment you suspect that a dispute has begun. If you have a good understanding of how the dispute started, the likely perspective of the other party and how you should respond, you will give yourself the best chance of success. The majority of contractual disputes happen when one side doesn't get the commercial value it expected from the deal. There are many ways this could happen – materials might not meet their description, service providers may not meet agreed Service Level Agreements (SLAs), payments may not match expectations – but the basic position is that one side hasn't got what it thought it would get. This isn't limited to contractual disputes of course. Regulatory disputes have similar causes: the regulator expects your firm to operate in a particular way and, in its opinion, you've failed in your duty to do so.

In the commercial world, when firms set up business deals they are usually good friends. There's an existing relationship, and often a sense of urgency and focus on getting the deal done. No one expects the relationship to break down, but this urgency can lead both parties to assume that everything will be all right. Complacency tempts both sides to skip over key details on who is doing what, when. This doesn't mean you should try to detail every possible circumstance that could go wrong; rather you should use the limited time you have to focus on the core scope and deliverables, to discuss the importance of the deal to each party and put in place proportionate protections to preserve each side's position. Be specific about what you will deliver, and when; be equally specific about what you expect to receive, and when.

It is the job of transaction lawyers to make the documents clear, to alleviate the risk of ambiguity in the contract; most importantly to ensure that each side is fully aware of their responsibilities and risks and the value they expect to receive. Litigation often focuses on flaws or unanticipated things in transactional documents – or ambiguities in law and regulation. In the commercial world, this is particularly likely if at some point one party believes the deal went bad for it, and now wants to try to wriggle its way out of it.

> The better friends people are when they do a deal, the messier it is likely to be when it all goes wrong! (Oliver Rule)

Note: You may not always be fighting your claim with the original party. Specialist claimant firms commonly buy up claims, and will then generally litigate more aggressively to monetize marginal positions.

Ninety-five per cent of disputes never make it to trial

Litigation is both costly and risky. It is for this reason that more than 95 per cent of disputes settle before trial. As any lawyer will tell you, however, a filed case has to be prepared as though it is going to trial because you can never be sure how receptive the other side will be to your requests to settle. You need to act as if you are willing to go to court to force the best possible settlement.

The 5 per cent that don't settle are often for bigger amounts, where the potential upside to one party far outweighs the costs of pursuing the litigation, such that even a weak case can be seen to be worth a punt. Whether you expect to find yourself in court or not, the approach to dispute management and strategy can have a significant impact (some say up to 30 per cent) on the success of your arguments. This statistic is experience-based, and we incorporate it into our litigation outcome calculator later in the chapter.

Three key sources of dispute risk: privilege, process and strategy

Disputes generally involve two conflicting views of a past event. There will often be factual discrepancies like what was said to whom when the agreement was executed or differing interpretations about, for example, what a document means. A good litigator will review the documentary evidence and material, zone in on the key documents, analyse each party's rights and responsibilities under the contract and identify what remedy is available to each party. When you assess your exposure to dispute risk, you should consider the level of control you have over documentary evidence and in particular on the preservation of legal privilege, the process that a dispute typically follows and the strategy that your lawyers might adopt.

Legal privilege

To best control information, you need to protect contemporaneous lawyer-client communications from discovery by the other side. Legal privilege allows you to withhold certain types of evidence from the opposing party. It is a particularly useful tool in litigation as it gives you control over information and allows you to time your legal arguments to best effect. How important privilege is depends on the contents of the evidence you don't want to disclose. Internal privileged e-mails, for example, may support the arguments of the other side – so it would be in your best interests to not disclose them. Having said that, if the evidence you are withholding through legal privilege doesn't support your own legal argument, you should probably think again about your current strategy.

There are two relevant types of legal privilege: legal advice privilege – covers communications between you and your lawyers at the time a breach occurs; and litigation privilege – covers communication that relates to the dispute, between you, your lawyers and third parties.

When to consider waiving legal privilege

Generally parties opt to maintain legal privilege in case a document is discovered that is harmful to your case, but sometimes, legal advice you get during contract negotiation can help your case. For example, if you obtained a legal opinion to cover valuation of assets in a loan agreement, the opinion might be evidence on which you would rely to support the value of your claim. You can choose to waive legal privilege within a dispute to disclose this evidence, but if you decide to do this you open yourself up to an unknown dispute risk. The other side is quite likely to argue that the waiver should apply to either all documents within a similar category, or to the entire body of documents related to the dispute. This argument is quite probably going to be upheld, so by waiving privilege over supportive documents you run the real risk of waiving privilege over other documents that may not be so helpful to your case.

Creating legal advice privilege for sensitive internal projects

Legal privilege can be particularly important when you want to protect internal communications on specific regulatory projects. Large businesses will often initiate projects to improve regulatory compliance that require a review of current practices and retaining experts to examine how robust their policies and practices are. The results of this kind of internal project can be used against a firm if a regulator begins its own investigation into the same area. In general, if there is potential for some investigation, you should preserve legal privilege to maintain flexibility to decide whether or not you want to disclose the report and the working paper supporting it. Non-privileged reports generated from internal projects – to review potential for anti-competitive behaviour, or adequacy of anti-bribery controls, for example – may be used by regulators to take control of the agenda and put you immediately in a defensive position. In practice regulators may put you under pressure to waive privilege over such reports, but at least you have a choice if you have taken steps to create and maintain privilege.

The UK courts support the preservation of legal privilege. In one case (see the case summary below), a large bank instructed lawyers to advise it on a regulatory matter. The lawyers reviewed documents and reported to a committee in a memorandum. The lawyers also took minutes of the meetings. When challenged, the UK courts found that the memorandum and minutes were legally privileged, as they were part of the continuum of legal advice. Although we will never know whether the contents of the memoranda and minutes would have been unhelpful to the claimant, legal privilege enabled the banks' lawyers to stay in control of the information flow on behalf of their client.

Case summary: *Property Alliance Group Ltd v Royal Bank of Scotland Plc [2015] EWHC 3187* (Ch)

The court considered the extent to which communications between client and lawyer in the preparation of such advice attract privilege. The documents referred to in the case were produced by the Executive Steering Group (ESG) of RBS in litigation relating to allegations of LIBOR misconduct. The documents fell into two categories: 1) confidential memoranda prepared by a city law firm, advising and updating the ESG on the progress, status and issues arising in the regulatory investigations; and 2) confidential minutes drafted by a city law firm concerning the discussions between the ESG and its legal advisers at meetings. These reflected the firm's views on the regulatory investigations, which were ultimately included in the minutes.

The court found the bank had engaged its external counsel in a 'relevant legal context': to advise and assist as specialist lawyers and communicate with regulators. That advice and assistance 'undoubtedly related to the rights, liabilities and obligations of RBS, and the remedies that might be granted against it either under private law or under public law'. Although some elements of the documents would not ordinarily have attracted privilege on their own merits (such as references to public events), here they formed part of the 'necessary exchange of information' between lawyer and client, the object of which was giving legal advice when appropriate. As such, these documents were privileged in their entirety. The court acknowledged that if the minutes had been prepared internally by the client's non-legal staff, recording the same mixture of advice and non-privileged facts, the documents might have been disclosable with the redaction of the legal advice.

The court also emphasized that there is clear policy justification for legal advice privilege being applicable to the flow of information between lawyer and client, including in the regulatory context. It expressly noted that, where there is a regulatory investigation, lawyers may need to brief the client on the factual situation to enable the client to decide what further advice to obtain and steps to take, or record the steps taken.

Although the judge emphasized a court would not uphold a claim to legal advice privilege simply because the documents were prepared by a lawyer, it is clear that by involving lawyers at an early stage in a review of your regulatory or litigation position, you can significantly limit the risk of being forced to disclose documents relating to that review in later court or regulatory actions.

The dispute process

If you fail to stick to court deadlines, you run the real risk of losing by default or, at the very least, prejudicing your position on costs. So make sure you know of and stick to any specific deadlines, and be prepared to follow a process roughly similar to the one below. You can mitigate the risk you will miss a deadline by outsourcing your case management to an external firm or by ensuring that your own in-house litigation team has a litigation management system similar to those used in law firms.

Note: Throughout the process the parties' lawyers will be writing to each other on various aspects of the litigation. Judges are rarely influenced by this inter-solicitor correspondence – and many find reading through reams of lawyer correspondence annoying – so we suggest you encourage your legal team to keep this to a minimum and adopt a measured tone throughout.

1 *Dispute arises.* As soon as you learn that a dispute may be imminent, inform your lawyers and try to preserve privilege. You will also issue a 'legal hold' or 'preservation notice' to preserve all potentially relevant documents. Remind your staff not to create new documents about the matter under dispute.
2 *Letter before action.* Detailed letter that sets out the basis for the claim, demands the amount the claimant wants to recover, and threatens court proceedings if the amount claimed isn't paid.
3 *Claim form and Particulars of Claim.* Formal documents that outline the cause for the dispute. The tone should be kept factual and calm.
4 *Defence (possibly with counterclaim).* If you are defending, generally your lawyers should be brief and provide a short description of your defence giving your position in response to the particulars of the claim.
5 *Reply to defence (possibly with defence to counterclaim).* Response from the claimant to the defence document.
6 *Case management conference.* This conference meeting sets out the timetable for the case. Not adhering to court mandated deadlines is serious and if you manage the case internally this is a risk to which your in-house team will need to pay close attention.
7 *Disclosure/Discovery.* Each party must disclose on a standard basis any document on which they intend to rely in court or which is relevant to their legal argument – whether it helps or harms their case. You can take a wide view of relevance, but only disclose documents that meet those tests. In the United States this can also include taking depositions and answering of interrogatories, etc. This can be an expensive and time-consuming part of the process, and is an area where many businesses encourage their lawyers to use e-discovery technology or other low-cost document review options.

8 *Trial.* Set date(s) on which arguments and evidence are considered in court.

Your dispute strategy

Even though 95 per cent of cases never make it to trial, never assume your case will not ultimately get there as you will be less prepared. Following the right strategy can improve your prospects of success by up to 30 per cent. In a $300 million dispute, this is a sizeable – and career-enhancing – saving. To get the strategy right, have a clear view of the key factors in a case.

> Get a clear idea of the strengths and weakness in your case early and where the case is likely to be won and lost. That way you can focus your resources most effectively and time any settle discussions to occur when your case is likely to be at its strongest. (Oliver Rule)

Best practice in dispute management

Litigation can be emotive. It is very difficult to stay dispassionate and rational when you have a personal stake in a case, but pursuing a case on instinct with little regard to the facts is a sure way to increase your risk of loss. Good lawyers will provide you with a rational view of the strengths and weaknesses of your case, based on their understanding of several key factors.

Establish the facts of the case

First you must identify the events that gave rise to the dispute as often this will be the most important factor in determining the outcome of your dispute. An initial focused review at the outset of your litigation will give you a clearer idea of the merits of your case, which should help you either negotiate a favourable settlement at an early stage or, at least, be able to approach your litigation from a position of strength. Prioritize the contemporaneous documents of central individuals in the key time periods under dispute, and put them in chronological order to get an understanding of the order of events, the reasons the parties acted as they did, and any misunderstandings that may have sowed the seeds of your dispute.

Be clear about the strength of your legal arguments

Even though your dispute may ultimately never be tried in court, the relative strength of your legal arguments developed for the purposes of trial will affect the settlement outcome, so the strength of your legal arguments can have a big bearing on your prospects of success. Before you launch into litigation, get your lawyers to give you a detailed assessment of the strength of your case, including an opinion from a QC (or senior advocate). If there is lots of money at stake, the QC's fees will be money well spent. His or her opinion will help you avoid the costs of pursuing litigation where the odds are stacked against you, and will also give you a head start over your opponent if you decide to seek early settlement talks.

It is ok to quiz your legal team about case law that will be relevant to your case and to keep them focused on your commercial perspective. You need to be prepared that case law may not support what appears to be a seemingly sensible commercial view as its primary aim currently (in the United Kingdom at least) is to protect commercial certainty in contracts. For example, the test of what contracting parties can reasonably be understood to have agreed, bearing in mind factual context (only mutual facts can be taken into account) known by parties at the time the contract was entered into, has changed in the United Kingdom. The analysis used to be very literal, but 20 years ago the courts started looking at what a commercially reasonable business person might think. Courts went from interpreting the literal meaning of the contract based on plain language and asked what makes commercial sense based on modern business practice. More recently, the pendulum has swung back towards the literal interpretation that the words in the contract are the best evidence of what the parties intended. This gives commercial certainty and freedom of contract, and means that when you negotiate your contract you should explain exactly what you mean to the other side, make sure your lawyers capture it in the contract, and don't leave anything to chance. The case review (*Arnold v Britton, 2015*) shows what can happen when you make assumptions about reasonableness in a contract.

> **Case review: *Arnold v Britton and others [2015] UKSC 36***
>
> This case involved a dispute between Oxwich Leisure Park (Park) which owned and leased 91 holiday chalets, and 25 of their lessees, about a service charge that the lessees were contracted to pay. The contract wording contained language that required the tenants to pay an initial annual service charge of £90 which increased at a compound rate of 10 per cent every year after the first year. A literal interpretation of this wording means that by 2072 (the end of the lease period) each tenant would pay a service charge of over £550,000 per annum. The tenants disputed this literal interpretation because it didn't make sound commercial sense.
>
> The UK Supreme Court upheld the literal interpretation of the original contract because in its view the meaning of the original wording was clear. The Supreme Court found that the principle of commercial common sense only applies where the meaning of the relevant provision is ambiguous. It is not a relevant consideration where the natural meaning of the language used is clear, even if this would cause commercially detrimental consequences.
>
> The moral of the story is: make sure your contracts say what you want them to say. You cannot rely on the courts to save you from making a bad deal or imperfections in your drafting.

Calculate how much is actually under dispute

Be very clear about how much loss has actually been caused. The other side may claim an exorbitant amount. Knowing the actual loss can totally change your perspective on how a dispute may play out. In many cases it will be important to instruct a knowledgeable expert witness (see below) who can speak about the events of the time. Consulting with an expert with the right experience at an early stage will help you to be clear how much you are really arguing about.

Locate experts with contemporaneous experience

Many disputes can 'turn' on expert evidence. The courts increasingly want somebody who lived and breathed the industry at the time, and has direct relevant experience of what he or she was talking about. You should act quickly to get the best possible expert on board. Even allowing for the fact that experts ultimately owe their duties to the court (not the party instructing them) you don't want to find that the other party has got in ahead of you and instructed the most credible expert in the market, leaving you with someone whose experience or credentials aren't quite right.

Witnesses may not perform well in court

Witnesses will talk about what happened and hopefully support your version of events. How well they perform under questioning, when someone is trying to trip them up, is a big issue. To identify individuals, search e-mails and phone calls and zone in on relevant documents. It's a good idea to talk to witnesses very early in the piece – even before claims are issued – to assess your prospects of success. It can be a really good shortcut to getting under the skin of the events and the motivations of the parties. A word of warning: if you're in litigation chances are something has gone wrong and it's likely that witness will give a favourable gloss to their recollection of events to justify their own actions. Don't fall into the trap of overestimating your prospects of success from the account of individuals who have a personal stake in the outcome. That said, if you can get on top of your analysis early from witness, documentary and expert evidence, and be dispassionate, you can give your client a really strong steer.

Be sensitive to the impact of a specific judge or court

Where your dispute is being heard is important as jurisdictions can differ greatly in the speed and reliability of the justice they dispense. Even in the more reliable jurisdictions, like New York and the United Kingdom, their quality can vary considerably from judge to judge. Although there is little that you can do about the judge you are allocated, it is a further litigation risk to take into account. If you're in arbitration you will often get a say in the make-up of your tribunal – but then again so will your opponent.

Disclosure/discovery and document review

Disclosure or discovery is often one of the first stages of litigation, usually after the parties have exchanged their statements of case. In England, if the court orders 'standard disclosure' (which in practice it usually does in large disputes) this will involve disclosing to the other side any document on which you rely, or which helps or harms your case.

The proliferation of electronic documents makes the disclosure process very expensive. It takes time and money to locate documents, upload them to an e-disclosure system, and for them to be reviewed by a team of lawyers. It's therefore important to discuss your document review options with your external counsel at an early stage. These could include doing an initial review in-house, using technology to cut down the scale of the review, and/or using a cheaper offshore provider to do a first cut. In England, parties are obliged to try to agree the scope of disclosure. This will include agreeing search terms, a date range and the individuals whose documents are to be searched. Parties are also required to estimate their costs of disclosure and to explain the areas where relevant documents may be located.

Disclosure is accompanied by a statement from each party explaining what sources of documents have been searched and, importantly, which have not. Parties also have to explain any problems that were encountered during the disclosure process and how they were resolved. This statement is usually signed by the in-house lawyer in charge of the case and includes a confirmation to the court that the contents of the statement are true. You'll certainly want to make sure you've been keeping a close eye on the process before signing so that you don't inadvertently perjure yourself.

If you manage the process well and comply with your obligations to the letter (including liaising with the other side where appropriate), you can avoid getting bogged down in costly and time-consuming disclosure battles and instead focus on the more important issue of how to maximize your chances of winning your case or obtaining a favourable settlement. Indeed many cases settle just before disclosure to avoid the time, expense and risk of the disclosure process, and lots more cases settle just after, because important evidence comes to light. If you can get an early handle on the documents and a clear idea of what happened, you should be able to avoid surprises.

Litigation tactics and approach

The tactics you employ to deliver your own strategy can also have a significant impact on your prospect of success. As a defendant, you may want to string out the proceedings, give as little information as possible, and force the claimant to make the running (and incur the costs). Later on in proceedings, if you are prepared to settle you may be able to make a tactical offer that will shift the cost burden to the other side if they turn it down and fail to beat your offer.

As a claimant, you are likely to employ different tactics. For instance, you may seek wide-ranging disclosure in the hope that documents will be uncovered that strengthen your case further. You will also care a great deal about the jurisdiction in which the other side's assets are held, and will give careful consideration as to how easy it will be to enforce the judgement if you win.

Similarly, you'll need to think about your opponent's motivations. Do they want to litigate this come what may or are they likely to be open to settlement? Are they being aggressive because they have a strong case or are they just trying to bully you into submission? Some professional claim funds rely on aggressive tactics to persuade large companies to settle a case just to get rid of the inconvenience.

Prospects of success

The above factors have a combined effect on your chances of success in litigation and they should all feed into any calculations you make about your prospects. This is important not just to guide strategy but to ensure that you set aside either provisions or contingent liabilities where required. International accounting rules state you need to set aside either provisions or contingent liabilities against litigation with a high or moderate probability of going against you. You will typically translate the 'prospects of success' for each of your cases into a 'likelihood of unfavourable outcome'.

Many lawyers, when they estimate the prospects of success, are very cautious. They are subject to loss aversion (a particular heuristic) and tend to add more weight to the potential for loss than they give to the potential gain. This can have a significant impact on the provisions you make in your accounts. Table 7.1 explains how loss aversion affects estimates of possible success. The conventional rating for prospect of success is in the left-hand column. We then

Table 7.1 The impact of loss-aversion on your 'likelihood of unfavourable outcome'

Conventional rating	Actual prospect of success	Likelihood of unfavourable outcome	Rationale
50:50	50:50	moderate	Lawyers talk about a case being 50:50 when they are genuinely unsure of the outcome
60:40	80:20	low	This is where loss aversion really impacts your ratings. 60:40 is bullish and means that you will probably win
70:30 (and upwards)	90:10	low	Anything over 65% means a win is likely, and is closer to 90%. But if a lawyer says 90%, then clients will hear 'I'm going to win', which doesn't leave enough room for the random elements of the courtroom
40:60	40:60	moderate	Natural caution means this is a possible loss, rather than probable
30:70 (and lower)	30:70	high	Loss aversion tends not to be a factor at this end of the scale. Anything lower than 30% is a probable loss

take account of the impact of loss-aversion to convert this to a more realistic 'actual prospect of success' in the second column. This analysis is subjective, so to be fully transparent we've included our rationale in the fourth column. The third column lists the 'likelihood of unfavourable outcome' that relates to the 'Actual prospect of success'. You would use this rating to decide whether to set aside a provision in your accounts.

Estimating litigation outcome

Because the projected impact of a case has implications for the balance sheet, you should use a litigation outcome calculator to verify your lawyers' thoughts on the probability of success, and minimize the impact of loss aversion and other natural human biases. Table 7.2 is an example of a calculator you can use to give an accurate estimate of the strength of your case. It sets a relative weighting to each of the factors discussed in this chapter, which you can adjust in conversation with your legal team depending on the type of case that you want to analyse:

- *Initial impact.* Select a value from the 'Range' that indicates how strong you are in each element. For example, if the 'Facts' were 100 per cent in your favour and backed up by contemporaneous documents, you could justifiably put '30' (as the top end of the 'range') as the score.
- *Range.* The potential range for your impact rating. The range varies for each individual factor, and if you decide to adjust the range values for your own calculator, make sure that they all add up to 100 to keep the maths easy.
- *Variable impact.* The amount that each factor could change during the dispute process, and to what extent the change could be positive or negative.
- *Comments.* You should document your reasoning, so you (or your successor) can revisit during the course of a lengthy litigation.

Table 7.2 Litigation outcome calculator

Factors	Initial impact	*Range*	Variable impact	Comments
Legal argument This will consider case-law, process, etc	*15*	*0–20*	0	*The legal argument is secondary to the facts and influence on outcome is unlikely to change*
Facts What happened at the time	*30*	*0–30*	0	*The facts are on our side and we have excellent corroboration from contemporaneous documents*
Witnesses How well do your witnesses support your version of the facts and will they stand up to cross-examination	*10*	*0–15*	–5	*We have good witnesses that support our version of the facts, but they could fail to perform under examination*
Experts How contemporary are your experts and how well will they perform in court	*5*	*0–25*	10	*We have not yet located a good expert witness, but finding the right one could substantially improve our prospects of success*
Judge/Court Past decisions of judge and locality of court	*10*	*0–10*	0	*The case is being heard in a court and by a judge with a favourable past record*
TOTAL	**70**	**100**	**–5 to +10**	**65–80 (your chance of success out of a possible 100)**

SOURCE: Based on an original version provided by Georgi Dimitrov Associates, with permission

How to offset the cost of litigation and transfer risk

Litigation funding is best described as the model by which an unrelated third party – the litigation funder – pays legal costs to commence and run a piece of litigation against another entity. In single case funding, it is usually used by parties initiating the legal action and, in return, the funder receives a share of any eventual damages paid out to the client. Funders usually want a return of one to three times their outlay, depending upon the duration of the investment and the perceived risk. As an example, if an average large-value case in the UK High Court costs around £1 million in terms of fees, it means mainstream litigation funders rarely look at cases in which the projected damages are below £5 million. So while it may take litigation off your balance sheet, it certainly doesn't come free.

There are three areas in which litigation funding can benefit your in-house legal department. First, the legal department budget for running litigation can often create tension between the finance and the legal teams. The use of outside capital removes the open-ended cash flow drain of funding a case. Because legal fees are paid by a funder and so do not affect business expenditure, it removes the negative effect of the external legal fees on profitability. The funds advanced are not a 'loan', but traditionally are non-recourse and therefore there is no balance sheet treatment of the advance. The funding remains off balance sheet.

Second, it is difficult to predict with accuracy the duration of a piece of litigation. This makes forecasting difficult, particularly when the proceeds of a successful case will be received. 'Monetizing' cases allows corporate clients to 'book' the receipts when they want. Any portfolio of litigation requires regular assessment and monitoring to ensure that the cases are running on budget and according to strategy. Using litigation finance is likely to incorporate a need for quarterly review and updates of the portfolio to the funder. This internal review and then external assessment means that the portfolio is monitored regularly and properly.

Finally, the most obvious area where litigation finance mitigates risk is in the risk transfer. Using a funder's capital to run the cases coupled with provision to deal with any adverse costs (in jurisdictions where there is costs shifting), whether by legal expenses insurance or an indemnity from the funder, means that the risk of running the legal proceedings is shifted in its entirety to the funder.

Like any other sophisticated financial service, litigation finance works most efficiently with diversified pools of assets, in which some investments may do badly but others will do well. For the funder, diversity lowers risk, and that translates to lower cost and a more attractive deal for clients. The increasing popularity of portfolio financing is indicative of a growing maturity in the field of litigation finance more broadly. It speaks to the fact that firms and clients need solutions not only for singular instances of financial need, but also to reduce risk and cost across a range of litigation matters.

The nine golden rules of litigation portfolio financing

1 *Portfolio financing is best used as a single investment in more than one case.* Capital is provided to a client that has multiple cases with one or more law firms. As in 'traditional' case financing, a portfolio investment is almost always non-recourse (in other words, if the underlying matters are unsuccessful, the upfront investment is lost).

2 *Matters within a portfolio don't need to be related.* Funders prefer diversity. When funding a portfolio with a client, the matters will of course be on behalf of one claimant but can involve multiple defendants in related or unrelated cases.

3 *You can include defence cases in your portfolio.* The costs of defending litigation can be included within the portfolio, as well as claims if the anticipated proceeds from the claims are sufficient to cover the defence costs. Alternatively, portfolios can be structured with bespoke definitions of 'success'.

4 *Portfolios can comprise any number of matters.* A portfolio may range in size from as few as two cases to all of a firm's cases run on full or partial conditional fee retainers, damages-based agreements, or a combination of these.

5 *Portfolio finance used to cover partial fees and expenses or expenses only.* One benefit of portfolio financing is the inherent flexibility to use the capital across a variety of different matters, where it is needed most. If, for example, it emerges that one matter warrants more spend

than expected, the client is free to use capital from a portfolio investment for that case, as opposed to another. Portfolio financing can also be used to monetize cases and as a source of funds for research and development or general cash flow. A litigation financier will advance funds to a client across a portfolio as long as the likely receipts from the portfolio sufficiently cover the outlay (and returns to the funder), subject to the financier's particular preferred ratio of facility provided to estimated value of receipts.

6 *Portfolio financing allows you to use capital flexibly, reduces overall risk and reduces the cost of capital.* Among the key benefits of portfolio financing is flexibility in the use of capital, as well as reduction in overall risk, which typically results in lower cost of capital. Portfolio financing is particularly advantageous for managing the impact of litigation on balance sheets and risk profiles; this can be hugely powerful for publicly traded companies.

7 *Funders look for diversity in a case portfolio.* From a funder's perspective, an ideal multi-case portfolio investment is as diverse as possible, with mostly uncorrelated cases involving different parties, different subject matter and different courts. As in any investment scenario, spreading risk across a range of matters reduces over-exposure in any one area.

8 *Portfolio investment terms depend on the number of matters, strength of case, and your own needs.* Terms vary depending on the number of matters included in the portfolio and the strength and stage of each case. As a general rule, capital will be less expensive on a portfolio basis than for any single case in the portfolio. A diverse portfolio reduces somewhat the risk of total loss of the investment, thus resulting in opportunities to provide more funding and/or lower pricing. Ultimately, terms are always based on the clients' needs. For example, if a client values certainty, the funder may structure the returns as a multiple of the investment or an interest rate-based return as opposed to a percentage of proceeds, which cannot be known until resolution of the matter. With portfolios, returns are often staggered as cases resolve at different times, so an interest rate-based return may be preferable.

9 *High risk matters are better financed as part of a portfolio.* Ideally, a combination of high, medium and lower risk matters provides a diverse portfolio. With particularly high risk matters, like patents and international arbitrations, a funder is likely to be able to offer better terms using a portfolio structure rather than single case financing.

How to analyse and manage enforcement risk

However you finance your litigation, one of the most important considerations you must make as a claimant is your enforcement risk – or whether you will get paid if you win. Even if you follow all of the advice in this chapter and eventually win your case, there are no guarantees that the other side will comply with the court's rulings and pay what is owed. For the unsuccessful party, whether to comply is almost always a rational commercial decision based on financial and reputational costs. On one side, the cost to the other side of evasion or other efforts to resist enforcement may be less than the damages awarded. On the other, the reputational damage that follows when you choose not to play by the rules could far exceed the cost of any single damages award.

It is difficult to predict analytically the likelihood you will succeed. There is little or no statistical data about how many judgement debts are honoured, or the levels of discount on face value ultimately applied. It isn't in the interests of claimants to advertise that their legal victory was a pyrrhic one that must now be accounted for, and lawyers tend to advertise only the fact of their involvement in cases that are legally or factually important, rarely whether they prevailed and never whether compensation was ultimately forthcoming.

No individual court or forum records ultimate compliance with its decisions. If they did, they would be reluctant to disclose incidents of non-compliance. It is in their interests to promote their venue as an efficient and effective place to resolve disputes. This lack of empirical evidence makes it difficult to analyse quantitatively – and benchmark – the impact of enforcement risk on your case strategy. The factors that affect your enforcement risk (or collection risk) are either systemic, or specific to your counterparty. Key systemic risks are choice of law and resolution forum. Counterparty-specific risks are generally related to the location of the assets, finances and reputational sensitivity. Analysing the factors, and in particular the interactions between the two, can show you enforcement risk.

Systemic considerations: choice of law and forum for resolution

Enforcement is one of many factors to consider when selecting your choice of law and forum for dispute resolution in a contract, or when structuring an investment. When considering the impact on enforcement risk, thinking about the worst-case scenario is a useful analytical filter.

For example, a United Kingdom-based claimant may consider that recourse to the English High Court is desirable for both predictability and cost reasons. However, a valid consideration is the relative difficulty in the enforcement of an English High Court judgement outside the jurisdiction. A relatively complex matrix of bilateral agreements as well as conventions and regulations (Hague, Brussels and Lugano among them) can be relied on, but the list of signatories to those instruments is largely made up of other common law and European jurisdictions.

Arbitration awards, on the other hand, are in principle at least more widely enforceable under the New York Convention. Its signatories include such dispute-heavy jurisdictions as the People's Republic of China and the Russian Federation. Domestication and local execution efforts may still run afoul of the local deficiencies in the rule of law, but having an award that is in principle enforceable immediately raises the stakes in a dispute and improves the chances of settlement. One note of caution: although the counterparty itself may be located in a signatory jurisdiction, its principals and assets may not be.

Whichever dispute mechanism is selected, enforcement will be much more difficult if your counterparty refuses to engage with the process. Rules are made assuming that people will play by them. Irrespective of the dispute mechanism chosen, if your counterparty refuses to play by those rules then enforcement risk will be much higher. For example, if the other side doesn't engage in the process and all you gain from the dispute is a judgement given in default, your prospects of getting paid are slim at best. Try to force the counterparty to engage in the process, and get them into a position where payment is the best option all round.

Counterparty-specific considerations

The impact of the systemic risks discussed above can't be properly assessed without information about the other party to the dispute. Never approach commercial disputes as purely academic exercises: the goal in such circumstances is never to create novel case law but to effect a dollar return.

The two most obvious areas to consider in anticipation of a scenario where the judgement debt must be extracted unwillingly are 1) the location and nature of the assets, and 2) the financial health of your counterparty. Most important: are the assets fixed, moveable or liquid in nature; and are they in a jurisdiction that will act on a decision of the forum provided for? Is your counterparty encumbered with debt, or being pursued by other judgement creditors with equal or perhaps better claims than your own? Any of these factors can both increase the internal cost of pursuing enforcement and reduce the funds available as compensation.

Less tangible aspects of a counterparty analysis include an understanding of its personal and/or corporate motivations. What factors can be identified that can be leveraged towards a settlement? Does it fear publicity? Would its own counterparties be dissuaded from working with it if a failure to honour its obligations came to light? It's also useful to consider who decides internally within the counterparty organization and therefore to whom should any overtures be made or pressure brought to bear.

Best practice in enforcement against recalcitrant defendants

Enforcement against a defendant that has done the calculations and sees the benefit in non-compliance is not for the faint of heart. To succeed, you need to be clear about your own motivations and commercial considerations, know as much as you can about the defendant, and have the best possible enforcement team you can afford. You also need to ensure that the opposition understands there is a way out of the current situation, and that it isn't fighting for its very existence. Existential disputes are fought, by definition, to the death, and that is rarely in your best interests (unless, of course it is a key competitor).

Mind-set and strategic direction

Perhaps first and foremost, your mind-set and strategic direction will determine the success of any enforcement exercise. At its simplest, the question is whether the enforcement is viewed merely as a loss mitigation exercise or as an investment in its own right. The former is characterized by a 'good money after bad' mind-set that condemns you (as the judgement holder) to making a series of disjointed and often sequential mistakes based on false economies. Perhaps worse, this mentality can result in stagnation or paralysis. As a counterpoint, the seemingly subtle difference of viewing the exercise as an investment allows decisions to be analysed on the basis of a return on that investment and for strategic direction to be maintained irrespective of the inevitable setbacks along the way.

Risk transfer and financing

As you've read, whether and how to enter into the prosecution of an enforcement strategy should be a rational decision. Emotion, often created by a sense of injustice and compounded by escalating and unpredictable cost, is rarely an asset in this complex environment; indeed it can skew the perception of the bottom line, and make settlement less likely. With this in mind and given the existence of a small and specialist market in the financing and management of enforcement cases, it can often be advisable to offload, in part or in whole, the risk of enforcement to an objective third party. This allows you to monetize what is essentially a contingent asset and outsource the case management efforts to professionals.

If you go it alone and invest your own capital, make a budget for the enforcement efforts, particularly taking into account the time it will likely take. Set a realistic budget that mitigates the feeling that money is being haemorrhaged and prevents asking for increased provisions. Establish minimum 'bottom line' settlement terms that you will accept in return for ceasing pursuit of a 100 per cent recovery. Because awarded damages do not always reflect actual loss, and judgements do not age well, setting the bottom line isn't easy, but it is important to set it before expending energy and budget on the pursuit itself. If you have no bottom line, you will at some point be asked to make a commercial decision at a time when you are least able to consider the commercial facts.

Employ a specialist enforcement team and maintain strong oversight of the process

Your advisory team will be crucial to maintain momentum and direction over the three to five-year period typical of most complex enforcements. The most difficult choice is often faced at an early stage: whether to replace the legal team that won the substantive case and use specialist enforcement counsel instead. There is no hard and fast rule, but there are very few enforcement professionals in the market, and trial counsel often has little or no experience in the area of enforcement.

Interview lots of counsel before assembling a top-notch team. The composition of the team may have to change several times in the life of the case as new factual circumstances emerge and the scope is refined. Whatever the team, keep a high degree of internal oversight and agree to a clear and robust line of reporting at the outset.

Tactical escalation and coordination

Most cases go awry because failures in preparation and planning (before the very first enforcement application is filed) result in drawn out and often costly remedial efforts. Once your enforcement action is underway, one question that will very quickly emerge concerns the appropriate scale and coordination of efforts. The two options are: 1) to attack the assets that are easiest to reach, and use monies won to fund further recovery efforts against assets more difficult to reach; and 2) to launch multiple simultaneous actions. There is no hard and fast rule as to which approach is best: assess the fact pattern in each case on its own merits. One factor you shouldn't lose sight of is that the opposition always has an information advantage. Any confidence you have that you know everything there is to know is misplaced.

CASE STUDY The DIFC courts mitigate enforceability risks in the Middle East

This case study explains the importance of matching contract jurisdiction to the location of assets. Loan agreements to Middle Eastern clients are often secured by assets in the Middle East. Many banks, when they loan money against such assets, will (often by default) choose London or New York as their jurisdiction in the event of a dispute. However, if the Middle Eastern counterparty defaults, judgements issued by London or New York won't be directly enforceable in that region, without the further expense of having to re-litigate in local courts. The cost of re-litigation and uncertainty about any local judgements mean that the assets are effectively unreachable and your loans are in effect unsecured.

The Dubai International Financial Centre (DIFC) courts can be used to mitigate this risk. The DIFC was established in 2004 to give confidence to overseas investors and encourage overseas investments in the region. The DIFC has mutual enforcement treaties with most of the other countries in the region, as well as other countries throughout the world (for example, China and France). The DIFC Courts have also created a nexus of memoranda of enforcement with other common jurisdiction such as New York, England and Wales, Kenya (access to COMESA), Singapore and Australia. If you make simple changes to documentation where loans are secured against assets in the Middle East, you maximize your chances of getting paid in the event of default – and ensure that your secured loan book reflects commercial reality.

Summary

When you find yourself in a legal or regulatory dispute, it can be difficult not to be emotional and make decisions based on gut feelings, rather than hard commercial facts. When 95 per cent of disputes result in settlement, making the right commercial decisions will save you significant sums of money. To give yourself the best chance of making the right decisions, you need to consider the different factors that might affect each potential dispute, and decide on the best possible strategy to minimize loss as a defendant – or maximize return as a claimant.

Expert litigators will take a number of different factors into account when they assess your case, and the skills and experience of a great litigation team can increase your chances of success by anything up to 30 per cent. Before you instruct counsel, get a good feel yourself for the factors they will consider and how they interact to inform potential provisions and contingent liabilities for your corporation. Don't be afraid to question your legal team about their expectations of success. The litigation outcome calculator described in this chapter will give a rough 'sense-check' to the gut feel that most litigators rely on. You could develop it into a custom tool specific to your own business, and conceivably use it to give better accuracy to the cases for which you must set aside much needed capital.

At the core of dispute risk management is the need to minimize the downside to your dispute portfolio. Litigation funding can convert litigation from a liability into an asset, remove it as a cost from your balance sheet, and can be a viable option if you are prepared to take a significant reduction in the amount you will win if you are successful. You need to make the right strategic decisions on which cases to pursue, based not just on the facts of the case and your likelihood of success, but whether you will be able to get your money back if you win in court. Assess the enforcement risk at the earliest opportunity – and absolutely before you decide on a strategy. When you decide to take out enforcement proceedings, think through the financial health of the other side, the location of their assets, and set a realistic baseline return at which it makes economic sense to bring proceedings to a halt.

Prevention is better than cure, but it is inevitable that at some point your legislative/regulatory compliance management will fail, you will find yourself on the wrong side of the changing legal and ethical landscape, or you will get caught in a dispute over a commercial contract or some aspect of intellectual property (that we will discuss in the final chapter). We hope that this chapter will help you plan ahead and implement a dispute risk management strategy that will help you make better decisions in the emotive dispute environment, and reduce your overall quantum of loss.

Non-contractual rights risk 08

Intellectual property: the gateway to your customer

Introduction

Throughout this book you've read a lot about how important it is to be proactive in your approach to legal risk management. This is particularly true where standard business practices tend to diverge from contemporary legal and ethical principles. This has led to huge exposure – for banks in particular – where standard operating practices are no longer thought to be acceptable by regulators. Intellectual Property (IP) risk is the reverse. Rather than law and regulation moving ahead of business practices, it is business practices that move ahead of the law as new incumbents disrupt markets. Traditional approaches to IP management often don't work when a sector is disrupted, and the position of IP is moving rapidly to keep up. The established approach to IP protects the results of expensive, time-consuming and isolated product development or innovation through filing patents or enforcing copyright, and is used as a way of protecting market position. This is being superseded in some sectors by contemporary IP management – where product development is the result of a shared connection with customers, enabled by digitization – and intellectual property rights are used to protect your brand (as the essence of your company) through trademark enforcement.

In some sectors, IP is quite obviously at the very heart of your business. Pharmaceuticals, clothing, high-end manufacturing and luxury goods all depend on innovation or brand. Even the financial services sector is on the edge of an IP revolution. New technology companies (Fintech) are encroaching on traditional banking areas like finance (crowdfund.com) or payment processing (Paypal). Emergent technologies like Blockchain could have a fundamental impact on the legal and regulatory work that accompanies banking and capital markets. Perhaps most intriguing is the way Facebook is positioning itself to enter the credit and payment markets. If you are a lawyer in the financial sector you will be looking at Fintech and Facebook with a wary and excited eye.

For the body of this chapter we have relied on the wisdom and experience of someone with far better background and expertise than ourselves. Deven Desai was the first, and to date only, Academic Research Counsel at Google, Inc., and he is currently an associate professor of Law and Ethics at the Georgia Institute of Technology, Scheller College of Business. Deven's research examines how business interests, new technology and economic theories shape intellectual property and privacy law. His work seeks to identify when those legal areas either explain restrictions to productivity in some sectors, or fail to capture society's interest in the free flow of information and development.

Digitization, decentralization and disruption

Risk as it relates to IP is often seen as a question of protecting an investment or protecting against the threat of someone copying expensive work. That misses a bigger risk: the threat of becoming obsolete if you misunderstand the limits of IP. Although IP used to be about one-way relationships between the rights holder and the world, in many industries that era is ending. Today, IP is more and more about two-way relationships, especially with consumers who are active and respond to your firm. In short, business and related IP must cope with the three Ds: digitization, decentralization and disruption.

That shift alters major assumptions about the nature of IP and the way you can exploit IP to create value. In this chapter you'll read why that is happening and how to identify when the way your business uses IP – and how your company relates to consumers – may need to change. You'll also read about some core assumptions about IP, how those views have become unstable, and how in some cases a certain IP, perhaps patent, will diminish in importance while the importance of another area, such as trademark, will increase. Most important, you'll learn what to do when faced with a changing IP landscape and the things you have to consider if you are going to use IP to your advantage if (or when) your business and industry evolve.

Digitization

Upsetting traditional views of IP

Some standard views about IP have merit and an intuitive appeal. One common argument that resonates on a gut level is that IP relies on labour and so it should be protected. People think they built something or worked on it, and so it is property and it is theirs (or the company's). From that view, anyone who treads on the property is a thief and the company, backed by the law, should stamp out such behaviour. Another classic but overstated view of IP is that without it, new ideas will be so unprotected that innovation will cease. In the simplest terms, the argument rests on the point that developing knowhow that might be covered by patent or writing a novel that would be covered by copyright has high costs to create, but once you share the knowhow or write that book, the cost to copy is low. IP law addresses that gap and the company, backed by the law, must go after infringers or the system will collapse. However, if you overcommit to these views or put too much reliance on a single sort of IP, you can suffer from the type of myopia that can destroy a business.

There are a couple of problems with these views. First, there are different kinds of IP, so rather than focus on a single aspect, you need to know which type of IP is at stake and how it works. In some cases patent will apply; in others copyright. Trademark will overlay your entire business and often protect specific offerings from your business, but you may also rely on trade secrets for aspects of your business that provide value but need not be shared publicly (the formula for Coca-Cola is an example).

Second, there is much evidence that although views on cost creation may be comforting, they aren't always accurate. The labour argument is overwrought, and scholars have shown the numerous problems with treating intangible property like physical property. Most creators draw on what came before as important inputs to their work, so arguments about property and theft don't hold up too well. Claims about high-cost creation and low-cost copying may be accurate depending on the industry at a given time, but certainly can't always be relied on as a barrier to entry for competitors in your sector.

A shift towards the consumer

Even within a specific area of IP, the nature of the industry – and what I believe is easily missed, the cost to infringe – play major, unstated roles in the IP system. Patents cover many things. Some have high costs to create (for example, pharmaceuticals) and some don't (software). Copyright covers books, music and videos on YouTube – all of which are relatively low-cost to produce and distribute now compared to in the past. It also covers blockbuster studio films that cost hundreds of millions to produce but are low cost to copy and share. The high cost to produce and distribute pharmaceuticals makes them expensive to copy for now, but the low distribution costs related to books, music and videos means that copyright-based industries have had to reconfigure to preserve their sector as their landscape shifted around them, and their ownership of copyright failed to prevent works from wide-scale unauthorized distribution.

The music industry was our canary in the coalmine. As the material, physical barriers to competition and copying behind music went away, the industry had to evolve or become extinct. It did both. The old, centralized, bloated industry went away. Labels shrunk. New players entered the market. Some labels and trade groups grasped at old models. As the industry resisted the new order of digital music, it sued its customers and argued vehemently that thieves must be stopped and lobbying campaigns sought to increase control over copyrighted materials. Yet, once labels embraced digital singles, gave up on copy controls and priced music so that consumers would buy rather than copy, a new balance emerged. Yes, the big labels are not as big, and the money has shifted, but the key lesson is that if you rely on the law to protect your business model, your business model is probably on its way out.

Despite the ease and proliferation of digital copies of music, it is difficult to argue that an entire generation woke up one day and decided to be criminals! This is simply an example of how contemporary business practices have had to keep up with the change in customer behaviour that is being felt throughout the digital world. What happened to copyright could easily happen to patents. Digitization has altered and will continue to alter not only the way companies use IP to protect their business, but also the way they relate to consumers. In simple terms, to understand these changes you need to think like business people and stay ahead of (or at least keep pace with) customer trends.

Decentralization

Altering and undercutting traditional business models

Until recently, companies were like broadcasters. They developed products in-house or acquired them and distributed them to consumers. Consumers may have had ideas about whether products were useful, or the way they were made, but that information was difficult to gather and may not have reached the companies at all. Consumers may have played with and rewrote a story from 'Star Trek', but few would know of that reworking. Consumers might have used trademarks for fan clubs, but they were local clubs. As digitization has taken off, this state of affairs has shifted and direct access to customer thought and action is unprecedented.

Digitization often leads to decentralization, and that change undercuts many business models. You've already read that copyright is the prime example, but there is more to say on that front. Many lawyers have argued that without IP and the copyright industry, creation of books, music, film and so on would collapse. Yet the explosion of music on YouTube and other outlets and of self-published books belies that claim. It isn't that garage singers and dubious writers did not create music or books before digitization; they simply didn't reach the marketplace. Today thanks to digitization and networked technology, they do.

As consumers realize that models other than those of high price and bundled goods are possible, they look for options. The VHS tapes price-point experiments are instructive here. As economists Richard Roehl and Hal Varian have explained (2001), in the late 1970s and early 1980s the home video market was for the wealthy. The price of the machine was high, and so videotapes were also priced at the high end. Once the price of VCRs dropped, people bought them to time-shift (record) television shows. That opened the door to consumers either owning or renting films on videotape. Studios disliked this idea, and in 1981 one rental executive described the studio approach as wanting 'total control of the cassette from the manufacturer to the customer'. Luckily for the industry it gave up on that model. The industry moved from high-cost tapes (between $80 and $90) aimed at rental store operators to $19.95 and lower for those who wanted to own a copy and watch a film over and over. By 1996 the rental market was at $9.2 billion and the ownership market was at $7.2 billion with more growth in direct-to-video movies to come. These experiments should have told copyright incumbents in music that lowering prices to make illegal copies a less attractive option was the best move. Anti-copying laws and technical measures played their part, and technology that hindered getting a clean copy of a recently rented movie probably helped the industry. That alone was not enough: the combination of a reasonable pricing and the fact that street or illegal copies were lower quality allowed a new market and revenue stream to flourish.

With digital music the fear of malware and a healthy digital marketplace, starting with iTunes and now including Amazon and Google Play, work to increase the supply of demanded music at market prices that make sense. In addition, new revenue opportunities have emerged as streaming music subscription services have entered the space, and live performance has increased as an important revenue source for artists. These changes point to another important shift.

Decentralization and disruption: new challenges and new markets

Digitization of music and other media has given consumers the chance to play with, remix and create works based on other work, and the command and control impulse of the old system is rubbing up against a new order. Fan culture – from mash-ups, to homemade music videos, to fan fiction – is challenging the idea that the copyright holder should control and charge for each and every way someone interacts with copyrighted material. The creation and success of YouTube illustrates the tensions perfectly. When YouTube was first created, on the one hand people were (and still are) enabled to create and share like never before; on the other, much of the consumer interaction with copyrighted material that was uploaded to YouTube offended rights holders, who demanded that the law provide legal options to stop these acts. Although a statute shielded YouTube from liability as a matter of law, millions of examples of potential and real infringement posed a problem. The dilemma YouTube faced at the time was whether it should stand on the law and a model that had allowed it to grow, or find a way to address some of these issues proactively while maintaining its legal protection and business model.

In the end, YouTube found an elegant solution with its Content ID offering that provided a solution to rights holders as well as 'infringers'. Rights holders had argued they could not scan the vast volume of uploads to see whether they might be infringing. Content ID works by scanning videos to see whether they might infringe a music copyright. To make that scan viable, however, music rights holders had to give a digital fingerprint of their songs to YouTube. Once they did, the scan could detect a potential infringement. If a scan detects that potential, a notice is sent to the rights holder who then decides what to do. Under the law the rights holder could follow a procedure to have material taken down – or do nothing. YouTube offered a third option: the rights holder can monetize the video with advertising and links to buy the underlying song. The upside to the rights holders was that in some cases songs that had been popular years ago jumped back into the top five for digital sales because of their newfound popularity on YouTube. This is a great modern-day example of how consumers can better interact with artists and share music, and labels can make money in a sort of micro-licensing that the centralized world of radio stations, ASCAP and BMI (licensing clearing houses) and labels does not support.

Disruption

New threats to patent-based industries

The lesson from the previous section is that digitization and network technology shifted the way music is created, sold and monetized. Incumbents throughout the old system felt pain as the industry changed, but the industry did not die; just one version of it did. That experience also has implications for patents and the industries that rely on them.

Digitization and decentralization have already started disrupting patent-based industries and they will continue to do so. Additive manufacturing or 3D printing has opened the doors of change to many industries that may have seemed impervious to digitization. The advent of low-cost, high-quality scanners and 3D printers and ever-increasing improvements in material science have already shaken a large range of industries, including the toy, gun, auto, car, pharmaceutical and aerospace industries, and it is likely that many other patent-reliant industries will face this change too. Several industries use versions of this technology to make better prototypes and bring new products to market faster, but something else is happening too. New players are entering industries, such as the automotive sector, where start-up costs used to be high and acted as a barrier to entry.

For example, Local Motors was able to use crowd sourcing to design a car with the winning designer receiving $7,500, and then complete the prototype in a little over two months. The two-seater has only 49 parts, most of which were made with 3D printing technology. The third production of the prototype took about 40 hours to build. The body itself is a one-piece carbon tub. One car reviewer noted that the other car he tested with a one-piece carbon tub body was a McLaren 650S priced at more than $300,000. Local Motors plans on releasing its first vehicle sometime in 2016, priced between $18,000 and $30,000. In addition, the approach of Local Motors allows it to build mini-factories for far less than the billion or so dollars traditional carmakers such as Tesla spend (yes Tesla is traditional on this point). That means Local Motors can adapt faster, deliver closer to consumers, and offer custom, high-quality, low-cost cars. In other markets, consumers and tinkerers are creating and sharing plans for homemade toys and even guns. Some of these creations are new and some build on offerings already in the marketplace. Like the copyright industry, industries that rely on patents are seeing small industry and individuals 'interact' with their IP much more than was possible just a decade ago.

Few industries are immune to these changes. Some may think that the truly precise and excellent offerings of their company and industry are shields. Consumers will not want shabby copies and, as many argued when I started looking at 3D printing and IP in 2010, 'The technology is not there yet, so there is no problem.' Tell that to Kodak and the film industry.

The rate of change in the technology that allows for what we can call 'The digitization and production of things' has been and remains fast. Scientists continue to improve the ability to use 3D printing to make items from ceramics, metals and even compound chemicals. Remember that we said cost to copy in pharmaceuticals is high for now? The United States Food and Drug Administration has approved the first 3D printed drug, and MIT has developed Pharmacy on Demand – a refrigerator-sized machine that can quickly change from a run of one liquid, generic drug to another. The hope is to one day add 3D printing technology and allow the machines to make pills too. Scanning technology allows someone to have little to no knowledge of design software, and yet create a good, if not exact, digital file of an object, and then use that file to print a copy of that object. With either exact copies of the original design files or quite good files created by a third party, more and more people will be able to offer a company's old designs or play with and offer new versions of those designs.

None of this is to say all is lost: instead, these shifts force us to think through where we can create and extract value. Technology such as 3D printing, synthetic biology, robotics, nanotechnology and more alter the advantages of firms; just as firms need to alter their focus lest they cling to areas where their advantage is fading if not gone. One way to think of these issues is that firms make sense when they make sense. That is, for some things firms are needed, because the costs to produce those things are high. When new technologies allow small firms and individuals to enter the space, that is a signal that the need for the large firm in that space is reducing. Instead of needing firms that can specialize and have a high level of division of labour, we see not just copying but increased production, new entrants and new offerings. A new network of smaller producers emerges. Thus if a firm is in an industry that relied in part on IP to protect the costs associated with its operations, that firm and its industry will be in trouble.

Beyond regulation and high entry barriers

The taxi and hotel sectors – although not usually associated with IP such as patents and copyrights – help us understand the deep way digitization, decentralization and disruption can batter incumbent players in an industry.

With high regulation and costs for both taxis and hotels, one might have thought there was no way to challenge them; yet with digital, networked technology both are facing competitive threats. The problems of coordinating and dispatching taxis; knowing a city's roads; managing rooms across a city, state or country; maintaining buildings and so on have acted as high barriers to entry to those markets. Those barriers have been lowered by the impact of digitization. The excess capacity of privately owned cars that sit idle most of the day or having a room or house to let can now be channelled through new, small business operations to consumers. AirBnb, Uber and Lyft tap that capacity so much so that the current market value of AirBnb surpasses large hotel chains, and Uber and Lyft have simply taken over the local taxi fiefdoms of old. Part of the reason is that the newcomers have not complied with laws that arguably apply to them; in that sense, the new competitors have lower costs. Another reason is that the costs of the old players can no longer be maintained. The rooms, houses, or cars are not digitized – as in turned into a digital file – but digitization allows a new platform to be built and everyone's previously idle human and physical capital can enter the market.

Cars also show us the dangers of thinking of digitization in only one way. As self-driving cars become viable and accepted, the digitization of transport will be complete. That change will press on vehicle-based industries thus showing that the equilibrium for individual drivers' ability to earn or even have a driving job will shift. The need for drivers with special licences, training or both to operate taxis, delivery services, trucks and public transport is likely to be superseded. As the costs of networking human drivers outweigh the costs of autonomous vehicles, the game will change once more. It is not just digitization, but decentralization and the impersonal nature of the transactions that matter here.

Responses: law and regulation return at scale

As the economist Douglass North pointed out, with impersonal transactions, costs such as the cost to know or evaluate a good or service, protect property rights, enforce contracts and share knowledge all increase (North, 2005). Our system uses regulations, standards, laws and courts to cope with these limits. As long as those costs are offset by a decrease in production costs, the trade-off works and the issues can work to a firm's benefit.

In a range of sectors the firm-consumer relationship has changed to consumer-to-consumer but not face-to-face transactions, which means that the problems of impersonal transactions remain. Going forward, firms that fill that gap will succeed. At first, digitization and related technology lower costs, and consumers rush in and connect with each other. Music, rooms, designs for toys or auto parts, and personal cars, are all shared or repurposed and often monetized. The laws governing a sector do not, however, go away. They are evaded until the service reaches a certain scale.

Once large enough, the reality of these approaches hits. A consumer grabbing a music file, renting a room, using a design file, or hailing a car, wants assurances about those activities. Does the file corrupt my computer or steal personal information? Will the 3D printed toy be safe for my kids? Will the room be clean? What if the owner has lied about the room? Is my driver a criminal? Does my driver have insurance?

Those offering these goods and services have similar concerns. Will someone pay? What if a guest trashed my room or house? What if a passenger demands I break traffic laws? Without repeat players and ways to address these problems, these offerings should collapse – but they don't.

Firms have entered and offered ways to manage these costs. Think of Amazon and eBay: both manage millions of small deals. The same is true for Uber and AirBnb. These firms connect dealmakers and create rules to protect both sides of the deal. They, like Facebook and Google, provide the platform that allows a large, interconnected system to work. What if your firm does not want to, or cannot be, the new, key platform? Platform plays are powerful but not the key lesson here. Again the question is where does your firm provide value and address the concerns North identified? In some cases, regulations – which are often held up as a problem – may be a saviour, because the cost of compliance will mean the firm can absorb compliance costs and still make a profit where smaller players cannot. In addition, certain parts of IP such as trade secrets and trademark will increase in importance.

Trademarks, trade secrets and the future of your business

If we assume that copyright and patents are vulnerable, because technology continues to erode costs that allowed those IP areas to work, to protect your business from IP risk you must seek, develop and use IP that is less susceptible to that threat. Two areas of IP, trade secrets and trademark, fit that role, although they too have limits. Secrecy can breed distrust, and while trademarks can help build and maintain trust, they are changing (like patent and copyright) because of digitization. Nonetheless, both areas offer options, and trademark in particular gives us a map forward.

Trade secrets in action

Trade secrets avoid a key problem of digitization, because unlike other areas of IP, trade secrets rely on not being disclosed. Trade secrets work by keeping the covered idea secret so the issues of investing in a book, piece of music or design file, offering it to the public for sale, and then having it copied and shared for almost nothing are not in play. AirBnb, Amazon, Coca-Cola, Facebook, Google, Kentucky Fried Chicken, Uber and others rely more on their respective 'secret sauces' than on patents for the core of the business.

Secret recipes, customer lists and so on must be guarded. If a marketing plan or customer list gets out, some of the value is lost. Even then, exactly how a company uses that information matters. For example, despite a historian finding and publishing what appears to be the ingredients list for Coca-Cola, exactly what proportions and which ingredients are still used today remains a valuable secret.

As another, broader example, a company's data and how it uses them is similar to Coca-Cola's secret sauce. Data-driven companies may have several things covered by trade secrets. The data gathered could be a trade secret; how they were gathered could be a trade secret; certainly the way the data are analysed would be kept close and secret. These secrets are the company's competitive advantage. Selling the data, the insights gleaned from the data, and the processes behind the service based on the data would undermine, not help, their positions. Thus it might appear all is well if one can rely on trade secrets, but companies that rely on trade secrets face problems that North identified, and we have discussed. In short, why would someone trust a company in an impersonal transaction when the main offering is explicitly a secret?

Ensuring trust and adding value through your brand and trademarks

As consumers give data or consume something they need to trust the company behind the secret. Food and drink must go through the Food and Drug Administration and its counterparts elsewhere in the world, and that process addresses safety and health concerns. So regulations, which are often decried as a hindrance to business, can fill a trust gap. Data, however, are less well regulated. As privacy increases in importance, companies that use data are starting to compete over the practice and reputation for protecting privacy. Apple, which relies more on patents and makes tangible goods, can make stronger claims about encryption, data usage and privacy. In contrast, Amazon, Facebook, Google, Netflix, Uber and others that rely on analysing data and using data to fuel dynamic, software-based services may offer encrypted services for shopping, e-mail, search and car services, but may not be able to take as strong a stand on data usage. Both positions are tenable, but their success relies on brand strength and in particular trust in the brand.

The more a company uses its trademarks to assure consumers that its goods and services comply with the law or offer authenticity that matters, the more its trademarks will work to keep a competitive advantage. Both 3D printing and copyright history help understand how this advantage works. Let's start with 3D printing and auto parts. Just as there is a demand for old and new music, there is a demand for old and recent auto parts. Vintage auto enthusiasts want original, old parts; having genuine or original parts matters for restoration. In addition, if you have kept a vintage car for some time and need a replacement part, you want to know that your mechanic is using a suitable, preferably the exact part, that your car needs. However, many vintage parts are no longer manufactured and getting hold of genuine parts to keep your car running can be difficult. Using 3D printing, hobbyists, mechanics and parts supply stores could solve this problem by 'printing' parts that are either out-of-stock or no longer in production. Even with vintage models, the automaker could be concerned that subpar parts are being made, or may think that even though it doesn't manufacture the parts itself, that third parties shouldn't be allowed to infringe the IP covering the part. For consumers, who will rely on that part to keep their vintage car safe and on the road, buying parts from a 'back-catalogue' offered by someone other than the automaker raises the problem of potentially defective vintage car parts, despite the seeming advantage of access to otherwise unavailable or expensive parts. Although the interests of the demand side and the supply side seem to be in tension, they present opportunities for manufacturers that are able to 'print' parts that are known and recognized as being of good quality.

This dynamic mirrors what happened with music and copyright. Some have argued that the music industry was too slow in bringing back catalogue songs and albums to market. As the industry fought to keep those items from being shared and failed to meet the demand, it created a backlash from consumers. Nonetheless, early swapped music files often had malware or were incomplete and so had a safety or quality problem. As online stores provided files that were safe and complete (and at a reasonable price point), consumers had more reason to buy music from online stores. However, unlike a music file that might crash a computer, if a car crashes someone might suffer serious bodily harm. Your brand, protected by trademark, can offer trust. Of course as you've read in the war stories relating to Volkswagen and General Motors earlier in this book, if your business loses customer trust due to some sort of legal scandal, the financial impact on your brand can far outweigh your direct financial losses. If the automaker addresses the supply gap and the trust gap, it has an opportunity to establish a brand that not only offers identity and other branding power but also goes back to a key part of how trademarks are supposed to help the marketplace – providing a certain level of trust about the goods and services to which the mark is attached.

Automakers and toy makers may soon enter or create markets similar to what Apple's iTunes has done. These other industries could open online stores to sell files they guarantee to be accurate and use those files to fulfil on-demand and custom orders, or they may use technology to stream the files to home 3D printers rather than letting the end-user have the file. That tactic would follow what Netflix does for film and television and Spotify does for music. In all these options, the company offering the file creates a market for the file and backs up the quality of the offering.

When a new company develops a reputation for quality and trust, it moves into a different dimension. When Uber requires drivers to carry insurance and conducts background checks, it enhances its service beyond coordinating transport and payment. If Uber does that as well or better than a local taxi regulator, Uber becomes a trust-broker much like Amazon and eBay have done for retail commerce. In short, trademarks can be powerful tools that allow a company to adapt to a digitized, less-controlled world, but they too have their risks.

Two dimensions of brands: trust marks and badges

Brands serve two functions: they help build and guarantee trust in the quality of your goods and services but they also act as a badge. Trademark law and older approaches to branding thought of the system as one-way communication that generates trust. As a mark holder, you offer goods and services and use your brand to communicate price, quality and brand identity. You can police against another company using your mark to pass off its goods as coming from you, but you can also use the law to enforce standards in your supply chain to provide the kind of quality assurances that customers will pay for.

For example, DeBeers diamonds protects its brand through a rigorous re-seller compliance programme. The DeBeers brand is built on two things: the quality (look) of its diamonds, and the source (non-conflict). It relies on its suppliers and re-sellers to adhere to strict quality standards and guarantee that they will not deal with unethical conflict diamonds. It enforces this through a costly, but cost-effective supplier compliance programme.

Branding has another dimension: some consumers want the brand as a badge. That is, they may want to have and use the brand but not the underlying good or service. That creates tensions about whether and whom to sue and what exactly your brand, protected by trademark, does for you in the market. Clothing brands help illustrate the problem. Consumers may want the LV label for Louis-Vuitton on a handbag, or a shirt with the Nike swoosh, but not care whether the handbag was really from Louis-Vuitton as matter of craftwork, or whether the shirt was made in a Nike factory. This type of consumer wants the brand as a badge, without worrying overmuch about the underlying quality of the product. In fact, as the ability to make an equivalent quality copy of that handbag or shirt improves so that few could tell the difference between the copy and the original, the desire for the mark becomes the thing sold. People are buying the brand label, not the underlying good. This case has similarities to the issues faced by the music industry that resulted from the ease of copying. Yet this case also has an opportunity that can be learnt from the lesson of DeBeers. If consumers continue to claim they care about how a garment or bag is made, that is with fair wages and no child labour, or in environmentally sound ways, the trademark can serve as a badge of corporate social responsibility (think 'Fairtrade') and possibly justify charging higher amounts because of that commitment to quality. You won't be able to fake this commitment. Unlike brand messaging of old, modern brands, which trademark law protects, also face the effect of digitization.

The 3 Ds and brands

Today, brands are channels through which you deliver messages about your company, but consumers also use that channel to communicate messages about your company. In the past, a company's ability to control a company brand and what it meant was strong. Brands worked as one-way communication channels. Companies used television, radio and print to advertise and deliver their message and while consumers had ideas about those messages and the brand, they were hard to detect and had little effect on the market. With the internet that dynamic has changed. Consumers can and do use brands to communicate. Those communications affect other consumers and in the end your company. Consumers discuss and police what a brand means with other consumers and also create fan clubs to celebrate and engage with brands; sometimes this in ways that deviate from your company's views. As Klein (2002) has shown, some people engage in activism by using a brand as the focal point to question labour, environmental and other social and political matters affected by companies such as Nike, McDonald's and Shell. As another example, the US company Chik-fil-A caused an outcry and suffered mixed market reaction when some of its officers took positions on same-sex marriage rights. Some consumers boycotted, while others rallied to support the company by buying more of its food.

In less fraught areas, for decades Harley-Davidson rejected the outlaw image for its motorcycles because the target market was suburban American men. However, once the company paid attention to the fan clubs and pop-culture images, it found that the outlaw image fitted with the target market and generated sales of a base-bike costing $20,000 and usually another $5,000 on Harley-Davidson accessories (Holt, 2004). Some dislike this change and argue that only the company should be able to control its brand message, but that view tracks the mistakes of copyright industries and the potential mistakes within patent industries. Although consumers may share negative or perhaps false views of your company, consumers who use the internet and your brand are communicating with you. They are communicating important information to your firm such as whether a new offering works, whether the price is good, and whether company environmental, labour and other social practices are a reason to buy or not to buy your offerings. In short, at a general level, digitization and decentralization have increasingly turned trademarks, patents and copyrights, into the gateway to the consumer.

Conclusion – IP as the gateway to your customer

As we said at the beginning of the chapter, the traditional concept of IP as a one-way broadcast is now outdated. When IP was mainly about business-to-business interactions, the laws about IP worked relatively well. Copyright holders licensed their content and infringers only mattered if, for example, they invested in stacks of audiocassette recording devices and sold those copies at swap meets and flea markets. With the advent of digitization all that changed. Anyone could copy and distribute a copyrighted work at scale rather easily.

The inventions covered by patent are just starting to face the effects of individuals being able to reproduce and play with those inventions. Trademark rights holders are finding that consumers can and do use company brands to question corporate practices and demand market action in the name of politics over pure profit maximization. Understanding this new order holds promise for companies going forward.

If an area of operation is protected by a given IP, and you find that the control and business model you used is faltering, that is a signal that your market has shifted. If digitization is at hand, ask whether that change moves control to more people, and especially consumers. That is a sign the decentralization is at hand. If your firm's power and value came from being a centralized place, decentralization means that time is over. Together, digitization and decentralization can mean that true disruption, as in replacement of the old centralized order and players within that order, is likely to be on the horizon.

Remember Kodak. When taking a picture required buying film, Kodak and other film producers provided a good that needed a centralized force. The labs and factories created new film media, processing techniques and chemicals, and paper. Consumers had to buy film and then take it to processing centres to see the results. Digital pictures changed that entire system. Rather than going to Kodak for film, and to processing centres to develop film and print it on high quality paper, people coped with poor quality digital pictures and prints, at least in the early days. It was easy to think that the new forces were different and that the quality of the new offerings would not keep up or satisfy customers. However, as digitization improved, the picture quality went up, as did printer quality. Those who thought that Kodachrome or Fujifilm had a lock on great pictures found that sufficient quality was good enough for most people, and soon it arguably surpassed those standards for all but the super-professional photographer. Put differently: digitization and decentralization lead to the democratization of an industry.

Many industries have been democratized. In music, thousands of artists share their covers and original work online. Labels can wait to see what catches fire or hunt for artists who might benefit from professional production. Film and television now has not only independent production but also new models for professional work. Netflix and Amazon use the power of lower costs and the two-way consumer relationship to test shows and see where they might evolve to be a hit series. Series can be the basis for comics, novels, action figures, and in some cases even theme park rides – all of which will still use IP to protect and license the offerings while also encouraging fans to engage and be part of the new worlds. Mattel and Lego are starting to allow users to design toys but have the benefit of high-end production. Cars are being designed by teams of distributed designers, manufactured and assembled in a matter of days.

None of these changes means the end of the firm; they mean a new era for firms. Firms can still be a wellspring of design, a source of trust, and a centre for community through and by which people connect and create value for both the firm and themselves. In many areas, IP is a direct touch-point with consumers, and when consumers start to interact and play with your IP you should pay attention. If you begin to fight with and alienate consumers over IP rights infringement, you may want to double check where value creation is happening in your sector. It is probably time to look to how you can create the things others cannot copy and play with easily.

If you miss the point where IP protections no longer work, you may miss the change in your industry that opens the door to that garage competitor who has taken over the office park next to you or even the one you are in. The biggest risk you face from IP is that you will continue to rely on and fight for untenable IP rights and business models as your industry limps towards obsolescence. The best way to manage this risk is to identify these changes early and use IP as the gateway to keeping an ongoing relationship with your customers as your industry evolves.

REFERENCES AND FURTHER READING

Bank of England (2000) *Oversight of Payment Systems* (online) http://www.bankofengland.co.uk/publications/Documents/psor/ops.pdf (accessed: 9 August 2016)

BIS (2011) Department for Business Innovation and Skills: *The Kay Review: Terms of Reference* (online) https://www.gov.uk/government/uploads/system/uploads/attachment_data/file/253465/bis-11-1015-kay-review-terms-of-reference.pdf (accessed 10 June 2016)

BIS (2016) *Standardised measurement approach for operational risk – consultative document* (online) http://www.bis.org/bcbs/publ/d355.htm (accessed 14 June 2016)

Bishin, W R and Stone, C D (1972) *Law, Language, and Ethics*, Foundation Press, Mineola, NY

Brand Finance (2015) VW risks its $31 billion brand and Germany's national reputation (online) http://brandfinance.com/news/press-releases/vw-risks-its-31-billion-brand-and-germanys-national-reputation/ (accessed 10 June 2016)

CCP Research Foundation (2016) (online) http://www.ccpresearchfoundation.com/index (accessed 10 June 2016)

COSO (2004) *Enterprise Risk Management – Integrated framework: Executive summary* (online) http://www.coso.org/documents/coso_erm_executivesummary.pdf (accessed 10 June 2016)

European Banking Authority (2015) *Final Draft: Assessment for operational risk* (online) https://www.eba.europa.eu/documents/10180/1100516/EBA-RTS-2015-02+RTS+on+AMA+assesment.pdf (accessed 10 June 2016)

Financial Reporting Council (2011) *Guidance on Board Effectiveness* (online) https://www.frc.org.uk/Our-Work/Publications/Corporate-Governance/Guidance-on-Board-Effectiveness.pdf (accessed 10 June 2016)

FSA (2012) *RCRO: Retail Conduct Risk Outlook 2012* (online) http://www.fca.org.uk/your-fca/documents/fsa-rcro-2012 (accessed 10 June 2016)

Guzelian, C P (2005) The Kindynamic theory of tort, *Indiana Law Journal*, **80**, pp 987–1036 (online) http://ssrn.com/abstract=619683

Ham, C (2009) *Health Policy in Britain*, 6th edn, Macmillan, London

Holt, D B (2004) *How Brands Become Icons: The principles of cultural branding*, Harvard Business School Press, Boston, MA

IACCM (2016) *Top terms in contracting 2013/2014* (online) http://blog.iaccm.com/free-resources/top-terms-in-contracting-2013-2014 (accessed 10 June 2016)

International Finance Magazine (2015) Brazil takes a $27 billion hit (online) http://www.internationalfinancemagazine.com/article/Brazil-takes-a-27-billion-hit.html (accessed 10 June 2016)

ISO 31000:2009 Risk management – principles and guidelines, ISO, Geneva

Kahneman, D and Tversky, A (2011) *Thinking, Fast and Slow*, Penguin, Harmondsworth

Kay, J (2012) *The Kay Review of UK equity markets and long-term decision making: Final report* (online) https://www.gov.uk/government/uploads/system/uploads/attachment_data/file/253454/bis-12-917-kay-review-of-equity-markets-final-report.pdf (accessed 10 June 2016)

Klein, N (2002) *No Logo*, Picador, New York

Limited, W (2016) *LexisNexis and BLP win 'supplier of the year' and 'best use of technology' at the British legal awards, legal IT insider* (online) http://www.legaltechnology.com/latest-news/lexisnexis-and-blp-win-supplier-of-the-year-and-best-use-of-technology-at-the-british-legal-awards/ (accessed 11 June 2016)

Loenstrup, M (2013) *The Puzzle Process* (online) https://thecontractpuzzle.wordpress.com/the-puzzle-process/ (accessed 13 June 2016)

McCormick, R (2010) *Legal Risk in the Financial Markets*, 2nd edn, Oxford University Press, Oxford

Mahler, T (2007) Defining legal risk. Paper presented at the conference 'Commercial Contracting for Strategic Advantage – Potentials and Prospects', Turku University of Applied Sciences, *Conference Proceedings*, pp 10–31

Mandelbrot, B and Hudson, R L (2006) *The Misbehavior of Markets: A fractal view of financial turbulence*, Basic Books, New York

Newman, J (2001) *Modernising Governance: New Labour, policy and society*, Sage, London

North, D C (2005) Capitalism and economic growth, in (eds) V Nee and R Swedberg, *The Economic Sociology of Capitalism*, Princeton University Press, Princeton, NJ, pp 41, 47

Purtilo, R (2005) *Ethical Dimensions in the Health Professions*, 5th edn, Elsevier Saunders, London

Roehl, R and Varian, H R (2001) Circulating libraries and video rental stores, *First Monday*, **6** (5)

SEC (2015) *SEC announces enforcement results for FY 2015* (online) https://www.sec.gov/news/pressrelease/2015-245.html (accessed: 9 August 2016)

Securitas Annual Report (2009) (online) http://www.securitas.com/globalassets/com/files/annual-reports/en/ar-09.pdf (accessed 10 June 2016)

Sky News (2016) *Norway's wealth fund suing VW over emissions* (online) http://news.sky.com/story/norways-wealth-fund-suing-vw-over-emissions-10284468 (accessed: 9 August 2016)

Standards Australia/Standards New Zealand (2007) *HB 296:2007 Legal risk management*, Standards Australia/Standards New Zealand, Sydney

Thaler, R H and Sunstein, C R (2008) N*udge. Improving decisions about health, wealth and happiness*, Yale University Press, New Haven, CT

Walker, D (2009) *A Review of Corporate Governance in UK Banks and Other Financial Industry Entities: Final guidance* (online) http://webarchive.nationalarchives.gov.uk/+/http:/www.hm-treasury.gov.uk/d/walker_review_261109.pdf (accessed 10 June 2016)

Whalley, M (2014) *Legal Risk Benchmarking Survey: Final results* (online) http://www.blplaw.com/download/BLP_Legal_Risk_Benchmarking_Report.pdf (accessed 10 June 2016)

Whalley, M (2016) *Legal Risk 2.0: Show you're in control* (online) http://www.ey.com/Publication/vwLUAssets/ey-legal-risk-2-show-you-are-in-control/$FILE/ey-legal-risk-2-show-you-are-in-control.pdf (accessed: 10 August 2016)

Whalley, M and Steen, M (2015) *Managing Contractual Risk: Insights from in-house counsel* (online) http://www.cbicontracts.com/wp-content/upLoads/2014/05/Contractual-Risk-Thought-Leadership-Report-Online.pdf (accessed 10 June 2016)

Wood, P (2014) *International legal risk for banks and corporates, Volume 1* (online) http://www.allenovery.com/SiteCollectionDocuments/GLIU_-_International_legal_risk_volume_1.pdf (accessed 10 June 2016)

www2.iaccm.com (2016) *IACCM – International Association for Contract and Commercial Management* (online) https://www2.iaccm.com/resources/?id=7619 (accessed 13 June 2016)

INDEX

Note: *Italics* indicate a Figure or Table.

Printed and bound by CPI Group (UK) Ltd, Croydon, CR0 4YY
16/09/2026
14963407-0001